A Particle of Light

A Particle of Light

Fay Key

ISBN 978-172-945-2325

Copyright © 2018 by Fay Key

All rights reserved.

No part of this publication may be reproduced, distributed, or transmitted in any form or by any means, including photocopying, recording, or other electronic or mechanical methods without the prior written permission of the author.

Scripture quotes from:
New Revised Standard Version, National Council of the Churches of Christ in the United States of America, © 1989. Used by permission. All rights reserved worldwide.
New American Bible, revised edition © 2010, 1991, 1986, 1970 Confraternity of Christian Doctrine, Washington, D.C. and are used by permission of the copyright owner. All Rights Reserved. No part of the New American Bible may be reproduced in any form without permission in writing from the copyright owner.
The Revised Grail Psalms Copyright © 2010, Conception Abbey/ The Grail, admin. by GIA Publications, Inc., www.giamusic.com
All rights reserved.

Printed in the United States of America

For my dear'sts, my community visible
ever blessed and ever blessing

For my family
in heaven and in earth

For green boughs everywhere

Contents

Prologue 1
1. Getting Born and Growing Up 5
2. Getting More Acquainted with Life 19
3. Into the World 25
4. Next Steps 30
5. I Will Lead You Home 38
6. Sojourner in the Land of Learning 42
7. The Story of Hospitality House 46
8. Lessons from the Best of Teachers: Hospitality House Stories ... 52
9. Days of Prayer, Months of Training 73
10. A New Life - Green Bough 76
11. The Houses and the History of Green Bough 82
12. Vision 112
13. Prayer 117
14. Community 124
15. Service 140
16. Amen 152
Postlude 155
Acknowledgements 186
Notes 190

Prologue

> I am obliged to bear witness because I hold, as it were, a particle of light and to keep it to myself would be equivalent to extinguishing it.
>
> Gabriel Marcel[1]

I sit here still and quiet in the presence of God. These stern and beautiful words of Gabriel Marcel touch something deep in the core of me. Wonder rises within me as I consider the precious gift of my life. I feel anew the obligation that comes with the gift, the stirring of desire to carry as sacrament the particle of light in me.

It was over fifty years ago that I first came upon those words. I had just begun divinity school. As a friend pointed out, I could not have perceived much of the meaning of the words at that time. I was in my early twenties, far too young and inexperienced to have much of a sense of their weight. Yet the words were important enough for me to set them down on the flyleaf of my Bible. Like some strange foretelling, a finger pointing to something as yet unseen, Marcel's words spoke to me. Though they were buried by the years, they lay in me, like hidden treasure, until I came upon them recently. I am sure that through the years they have been a part of the Holy Spirit's secret guiding of my life.

A Particle of Light

What a privilege to hold a particle of light—and not only to hold it, but also to spread its radiance, showering that bit of light all around. This is a direct gift of the Creator who sees and loves the creature, who sets within the creature the divine fire of creativity. This is the Light of Christ, and we are its earthen vessels.

I carry a spark of light—and I am grateful to the Giver! A particle of light is entrusted to each of us, a sacred gift from beyond. We are responsible for the light we carry. Jesus our Light says to us all, from the least to the greatest, "You are the light of the world. Shine."[2]

Obliged to bear witness, I must, then, tell my story. For years people have encouraged me to write this story, and though I have been slow to take up such a daunting task, I have felt in my own deep self an urgency to write it. In many ways this is a simple story of being loved and of loving, a story of call and response. It is a story of being given a treasure to carry, a task to complete. One morning a couple of years ago I awoke with a dream fresh in my mind, and I knew it was time to write.

I was walking along a lonely country road carrying a baby in my arms, a child nearing his first birthday. I loved him. In the dream I was not sure where the child had come from, but I had been carrying him for a long time and knew I was to carry him to a far place, the name of which I could not remember. The child was so good. He lay against me, sometimes sleeping, sometimes awake and engaged with the world of nature around us. Now and then I felt the weight of him, but when I flagged he would become light, and I went on in joy and purpose. I walked with him along the country road for a long way, until we came to the edge of a town. I turned onto a street with small shops and businesses along the right hand side and a green, grassy field with trees on the left.

The place had the feel of an old-world village. I went into a small tavern full of people, sat down at a long table and ordered something to eat and drink. A woman sitting in the chair to my left asked if she could help me. I told her I was looking for the place I was to take the child and thought it was in this town, perhaps just up the street, a tavern as well. I could not remember the name of the meeting place, but she knew where it was and told me it was only a few doors away. I saw a young man with long hair and vibrant energy. I recognized him as the father of the child. When I got up to leave I was not sure he would follow. But as I walked into the street I looked back, and he was running to catch up with me. I was happy to see him coming to take responsibility and help us get to our destination. He walked alongside me and offered to carry the baby the rest of the way. I handed the child to him, and the three of us went along until I saw the doorway of the place where we were to meet the one to whom I was taking the child. I knew I had accomplished what I had been asked to do and felt deeply grateful and relieved. The dream ended before I entered the door. I awakened with a feeling of joy. My first thought on waking was that this dream was about my writing the story given to me from before I could remember, the story I was to carry to the place where it is meant to be.

I hold a particle of light, and I am obliged to bear witness.

Now 76 years old, I am writing from the Anchorhold, my little dwelling at Green Bough House of Prayer, where I have lived in contemplative community for the past thirty years. Each night I walk to my house under the dark canopy of sky. On clear nights that sky is spangled with stars and a moon. Though the moon is lovely in every phase, I admit partiality to the silver crescent with a bright planet floating only a thumb-width away from it. Only in the darkness are moon and stars revealed. Though we cannot see the sun at night, it is present, lighting those "far distant isles" with its light, so that they bear witness to the light they reflect. Looking up, out into vast and timeless space, I sense a strange intimacy. *I am.* Bound by the particularity of my own time and space, I feel the wonder of being alive, of being a small part of something infinitely big. I feel the mystery of each small *I am* echoing, reflecting, held in, loved by, the big I AM. Nearly every night I say aloud, "I would not have missed this journey in earth for anything! Thank You."

Daily I encounter the Was-Is-And-Ever-Shall-Be that sits hidden, elusive and patient at the center of life, informing, reforming, conforming, transforming everything if only we consent to be attentive. The One whose light we carry attracts and engages us in the lively struggle of *relationship*—speaking, listening, guiding, scattering, gathering, shattering, shaping each of us in ways beyond our comprehension—calling us each to become more than we ever dreamed we could be. My pathway has held many unlikely meetings, connections, signposts along the way. I am in awe as I reflect on the special events, places and people who have been a part of the path that led me to Green Bough House of Prayer and a life in blessed community here.

Chapter 1

GETTING BORN AND GROWING UP

For it was you who formed my inward parts;
   you knit me together in my mother's womb.
I praise you, for I am fearfully and wonderfully made.
   Wonderful are your works; that I know very well.
My frame was not hidden from you,
   when I was being made in secret,
   intricately woven in the depths of the earth.
Your eyes beheld my unformed substance.

                              Psalm 139:13-16a[1]

Where does life begin? Where does *a* life begin? "In the beginning," begins our story. Back there among the morning stars, back there where chaos was first being ordered and creation called forth, uncountable years ago, before there was time, in the beginning. God was breathing and laboring. Somewhere along the way, God, fumbling in the darkness cried out, "Let there be light!" The story goes on to say, "and there was light, and God saw...." I imagine God saying, "Let there be light! I want to *see* what I am doing! I want to see my creatures." God sees, and all is held in the Eye of God—the very eye that beheld my unformed substance. We are the sparkles of God's eye. God sees, and the Divine Heart is stolen by the creature. "Very good! Beautiful!" God proclaims.[2] Teresa of Avila says that prayer is "looking at the one who is looking at me." If we look, we see looking back at us the eye of a lover; we see *God in love*! And if we listen we hear the Lover saying, "You are the apple of my eye—my loved one from the beginning." Of course, God says this to every single creature…past, present and to come. God has said this to me.

I was a breech baby, endangering the life of my mother. On March 30, 1942, as my father stood in the doorway of the hospital delivery room, the doctor told him that he was not sure he could save both my mother and me, but somehow we both survived. As I was growing up my mother would tell me occasionally that I was alive for some special purpose. I believe this is true for everyone, and the circumstances of my birth gave emphasis to this for me.

I was born into a world at war. As I was told the story, the Sunday afternoon of December 7, 1941, was quiet and warm in the way early December in middle-Georgia can be. Doors and windows were open. My father and mother, Woody and Martha, were sitting in the swing on the front porch of my Key grandparents' house in Adrian, Georgia. My mother was pregnant with me, who would be their firstborn. Just inside the door the radio was playing. Suddenly the regular programming was interrupted by an announcement that the Japanese had bombed Pearl Harbor. A chill spread over the warm day. My father always said that his first thought that afternoon went to the child in his wife's womb. Would he ever see that child? Would he ever know his offspring? His heart sank as he thought of having to go to war. He loved me and prayed for me from the moment he knew I was a living being. I was born on the Monday of Holy Week, and as it turned out, he had several months with us before he became a Merchant Marine and sailed off into the darkness of war.

Getting Born and Growing up

During these months we lived in Swainsboro, Georgia. My father worked for a furniture store, and in the evenings he delivered furniture all over town. My mother and I must have ridden with him often. I grew up having many people tell me that when he delivered furniture to their house he would say to them, "Now come out and see my baby girl." He would take me out of the truck, hold me in the beam of the headlights and say, "Isn't she beautiful." I was always sure everybody said "Yes." What better story could a child be told than the simple story of being loved, cherished as a beautiful human being. Through human love I was shown early that this was the way our Creator sees us. Beautiful, everyone. And it is how God wants us to see one another.

The Keys

The Key side of my family was Methodist, going back several generations. I grew up hearing stories of my great-great-grandpa Ches Flanders, who was a lay Methodist preacher in Emanuel County following his service in the Civil War. From all accounts he was a beloved and spirited person who preached and prayed with the booming voice of a prophet—and who, from time to time, could "cuss a blue streak." I imagine him as a good country man, strong, hardworking, rough and gentle, with a wide stubborn streak and a heart given to God.

The Grandpa Ches story that affected me most was told to me in this way: He would often rise up from his bed in the night, kneel down and pray for the seed of his loins, that through the ages they might love and serve God. Now, I had no idea what 'the seed of his loins' meant, but I knew it had to do with me. And so, I say it was Grandpa Ches who ordained me, over a hundred years ago. From his lineage came many faithful Christians both lay and clergy—stubborn and with hearts given to God.

My Key grandparents, Morris and Bertha, were poor and poorly educated. My grandmother finished seventh grade. My grandfather stopped school at fourth grade. He could barely read and write. There was a homespun wisdom in them. They were humble, honest, hardworking people. My grandmother cared for the house and children. My grandfather ran a small restaurant in Adrian. As a child my father worked alongside his father in the restaurant, washing dishes, serving meals to customers, cleaning up. They barely made ends meet; then the great depression forced my grandfather to close his business, leaving the family in difficult financial circumstances.

Their moral undergirding was formed by a deep religious faith. Daily prayer and Scripture reading were at the center of their family life; Methodist piety fashioned them warm hearts. There is a story about my Granddaddy Key that I always loved to hear. I was the first grandchild in the family, and he loved to hold me. I was told that when we would come to visit them, I would hold out my arms and say, "Granddaddy, take your baby." One day a little black girl, who was being chased by some big boys, ran frightened and crying through the screened door of the cafe, straight to my grandfather. He scooped her up in his arms and made the boys leave her alone. When he put her down, a white man, standing there watching the incident, said to him, "Well, Morris, how did that little colored girl feel in your arms?" My grandfather said, "She felt just like my little granddaughter Fay."

THE CARTERS

My mother was a Carter who grew up in Scott, Georgia. My Carter grandparents, Marvin and Debbye, were Methodists also. They were not wealthy, but they had enough of this world's goods to live comfortably.

Getting Born and Growing up

And they were better educated than the Keys. After attending the University of Georgia my grandfather, who loved the land, returned to Scott to live out his days as a farmer and surveyor.

My grandmother went to Wesleyan College in Macon in the early 1900s. She was there at the outbreak of the influenza epidemic in 1918. Notified that several members of her family in Hagen, Georgia, were sick and that she was needed at home to help care for them, she packed her things, rode the train home, saw her family through the crisis and never returned to school.

She married my grandfather who was 13 years her senior with three children from a previous marriage. Her only child was my mother. Soon after I moved to Scott to start Green Bough House of Prayer, I found her wedding ring in a box of trinkets. I found it on what would have been the sixty-eighth anniversary of their wedding. My grandfather always called her, "Wife," or "Mrs. Carter." She referred to him as "Mr. Carter" or "Mr. Marvin." I called them Papa and Ma Carter.

When I was little and Papa would announce that he was going out to the field, I often begged to go with him. Ma Carter would say, "No. You can't go. That's too far for you to walk. You'll be tired and miserable." I would continue to beg; my grandmother would continue to say no. Finally Papa would say, "Wife, let her go." So off my grandfather and I would start. Sure enough very soon I was tired. My feet hurt. I was hot. I was whining about having to walk so fast. My grandfather would turn around and pick me up in his arms and carry me all the way to the field and then back home. His kindness was an early lesson in grace, the sheer gift of love, undeserved, unconditional. I experienced God's promise enacted: "You have been borne by me from your birth, carried from the womb; even to your old age I am he, even when you turn gray I will carry you."³

While my father was away during World War II, my mother and I lived with my grandparents in Scott in the house now called the Herb of Grace, a part of Green Bough. I have good memories of living in that house. I have a sense that not only the people there, but the place as well, loved me. The road in front of the house was still a dirt road. Occasionally I would see black women walking along the road with baskets or bundles balanced on their heads. They were probably carrying laundry or staples for cooking. That was the early 1940s, so some of them were likely only a few generations away from slavery. Life would have been very hard for them. Segregation was a fact of life, and the divide was great. Watching those women who walked along the road, I had no idea of the awful southern evil that kept such distance between us. As a sheltered child, three or four years old, I could not make much sense of the situation. I had only a vague sense of 'something.' It would be a few years before I knew the word *inequality* and learned something of its effect.

At the war's end there was a collective sigh of relief and gratitude. People's lives were interwoven, sorrows and joys were mingled. The wounds of war affected everyone. In peace, people learned what it meant to mourn with those who mourn and rejoice with those who rejoice. For some families peace meant facing the wrenching loss of a dear one who would not be returning. For other families peace meant the joyous homecoming of some loved one who had been away for a long time. For me it was my father who was coming home.

Getting Born and Growing Up

My Parents

My parents were dating while they were still in high school. My father, two years older than my mother, was working at a furniture store when my mother graduated. She went off to college in Statesboro—Georgia Teachers' College as it was known in those days. She disliked it from the start. At the end of the first quarter she left school, and she and my father eloped on January 12, 1941.

I think my parents had a good marriage. They respected one another, were faithful to their vows and lavish in their affections toward each other and their two children. They loved in action. Their love was in the living of their days; in their faithfulness; in their honoring of marriage; in their life together in the context of a larger community of family, church, town, world. In that wonderful old phrase, "they gave of themselves." They had their share of differences and disappointments, of course, but they were present to one another and to others.

My father was something of a "straight arrow." He worked hard all his life and felt somewhat lost in his retirement years. Having grown up with very little materially, he was accustomed to living simply. All his days he was moved by poverty, and he did not shield me from the suffering of people. When I was a child he introduced me to people who lived in dire poverty; there were many in the late 1940s. From time to time my mother helped me choose some of my clothes and toys, and my father took me to visit some family in a hauntingly poor house so I could share them with the children there.

He never forgot the day during the great depression when his father closed his little cafe, padlocking the door one morning and walking away with nothing. My father always felt the sadness of that day and remembered his father's anxiety as the two of them, feeling the weight of fear and uncertainty, walked down the dirt path to their home.

My mother was fun-loving, light-hearted and deeply sympathetic. She knew how to laugh and how to weep. She often said, "Being cheerful is your duty. You can lift someone's spirits with a smile and a greeting." She was an excellent listener and taught me how to listen. She grew up on a farm and though she loved the land, she never wanted to stay on the farm. She wanted to be a nurse, but her father would not agree to that.

After marriage my mother worked alongside my father in the clothing business they established. She found an outlet for her caregiving skills by helping establish a volunteer program and a gift shop at the Emanuel County Hospital. She was often called to be with families who were worried or grieving and would go to the hospital day or night to be with them.

Self-giving was a way of life for Mama, and she did her best to teach me that way of living. She knew the truth of the paradox that lies at the heart of faith: *To give is to receive.* One of the strongest lessons she taught me came at the end of my freshman year at Emory at Oxford. I took a summer job at a Methodist Church in Macon. I did not own a car, so my mother drove me there to look for a place to live. Within walking distance of the church we found a bargain—a five-dollar-a-week room in the home of a woman who seemed to me to be centuries old. The house was dark and dirty, and I felt uneasy about the prospect of living there. After a look at the bathroom, crusty with filth, I knew this was not the place for me. I kept waiting for my mother to say, "This is not good enough for my daughter." Instead, she gathered some cleaning supplies, got down on her knees and scrubbed that bathroom. As she finished cleaning the tub she said to me, "You can help this woman if you want to." I stayed there all summer. The dirty, old house became dear to me, and I grew to love the old woman, who every morning in her dirty kitchen, cooked us each an egg for breakfast, all the while singing in her cracked voice, "I'm only a bird in a gilded cage…." I do not yet know if she sang as she cooked or cooked as she sang, but I do know that she helped me. My mother knew that was the way it would be.

To this day, when I see a bathtub I hear that clear challenge: "You can help if you want to." And I praise God, because I know in some inexplicable way that means that I, too, will be helped. To give is to receive. To die is to live. That is the faithful Word of our faithful God, spoken to me by my faithful mother.

She died in 1985. It was the closest relationship I had had with death—a huge loss, but I did not find death frightening. On the day of her death she called my father and her best friend Helen (whose husband had died two years earlier), into her room and asked everyone else to leave. She then told them that they should get married and take care of one another. She had told me she was going to do this, and my response to her was, "You can't do that." She said, "Yes, I can. Your daddy will not know what to do without me. They need one another. It will be good for them." It was one of the most selfless acts I can imagine. It freed them to take care of themselves, pick up their lives and move on.

She died of bone cancer on December 21, 1985, after nearly two years of suffering and valiant struggle. A roomful of family and friends were gathered around her hospital bed as she died. We held her as she drew a last blessedly peaceful breath. She was lucid to the end. She looked at us all, as if in blessing, and then the light faded from her eyes. We wept, gave thanks, and prayed. Christmas had come early for her.

During the long, painful illness someone wrote me that her suffering was a ministry. Being with her and the rest of my family at the end, I came to understand a little better what that meant. We all want and need to be close to the awesome events of life, to touch the edge of Mystery and be assured that at the center all is well. My mother had the humility to let people share in her suffering and dying. She would say to us, "Leave the door open." And people came into her room day and night—to see, to touch, to find strength and peace. She gave us her wounded self and so made us more aware of the wounds of others. She gave us her broken body and so called us to a deeper commitment to live as Christ's compassionate people in hope that through our wounds others might be healed. In her dying new life came.

We buried her on December 23. For the processional hymn we sang, "Hark! The Herald Angels Sing." The church was packed with people, and the singing buoyed us. We were floating on music. When we reached the words: "Light and life to all he brings, risen with healing in his wings," I felt lifted up in peace and joy. I felt the weight of her body, by the end a bag of flesh filled with crumbled bones, grow light. Pain fell away. And there was the brief though enduring 'understanding' that she was healed, restored. Light and life were hers by the grace of the One who is risen with healing in his wings. I was clear that sorrow and joy are of a single piece, tightly braided in our lives, like death and life, Cross and Resurrection.

My father died years later on July 26, 2005. He and Helen had a good marriage of 19 years, and we buried him on July 29, Feast of St. Martha.

Getting Born and Growing up

My mother's name was Martha, and I felt as though all the saints were gathered around as she welcomed him home. As my father drifted into dementia, he never lost the deep essence of himself. His mind failed, his body declined, his outer world narrowed—and yet his face was merry, his eyes twinkling. What grace to have twinkling eyes in the days of diminishment: Light shining in the darkness; Christ in our poverty; the Baby lying in the Manger. The wonder of life and sweetness embedded in the dry, prickly, uncomfortable straw of aging!

As he grew weaker my brother and I worked together with Helen trying to ease the load, hoping we would not have to put him in a nursing home (though finally we did). I spent most nights with them during this time. The two of them always had a morning devotional reading and prayer before breakfast. I joined them when I was there. One morning we were sitting quietly at the table, getting ready for their morning reading. Suddenly my father spoke in his trembling, old voice, "Out of the depths I cry to you, O Lord. Lord hear my voice!"[4] He was quoting from Psalm 130, which was the Psalm appointed for that day's reading. He could not have known that. Helen and I were in awe.

On the morning following his death, I went to get us biscuits for breakfast. When I returned Helen said, "Come here, I want to show you something. I've never seen anything like it. It's a moth." And there hanging on the outside of the kitchen window was a very large moth. Its wingspan must have been six inches. We marveled at the size and beauty of it. The pattern on the wings looked like ranges of mountains one behind the other, fading off into the distance. The colors were deep—brown, blue, green, mauve. I told Helen that I had read that the moth is a symbol of death. It transports the soul of one who has died to the other side. So we took it as a visitation from my father, who had come to breakfast with us one last time before departure. It hung there, wings folded, and let us feast our eyes. It felt like a gift of reassurance. We called my brother Denny to come and see. And we asked a neighbor to come with her camera. When we told her what we thought of it, she said, "That's just like Woody."

It is hard to watch those we love depart this life. On the night of his dying several of our family were gathered around his bed with our hands on his tired, frail body as he crossed the Jordan. It is an awesome feeling to stand in the presence of such Mystery—and to know it as good. He and we were as ready as humans could be for such a profound letting go. Even so we felt the heavy weight of sadness. I believe that the veil between this world and the next is very thin and am thankful for that "mystic sweet communion with those whose rest is won." I ask daily for the prayer of heaven for those of us who journey in earth.

Nearly a year after his death I dreamed of my father. In the dream I was looking for him. When I found him I said, "There you are, and you're looking good." We hugged. Light was in and around him. He was wearing a yellow shirt and was fresh and beaming. He held a card cupped in his hand and I looked over the top to see what was written on it. I couldn't make the words out, and he moved his hand around so I could see. At the top of the card was written "Healing takes time." When I awoke I felt deep happiness. I can't remember ever seeing my father wearing yellow, so I looked up the color and found that it represents wisdom and life energy. As I began to write this dream down, I realized that it was the first day of summer. Time had passed. It seemed that in the night there was another turning. I had passed into a new season of life. Summer had come again with its invitation to slower-paced, more reflective days. I found myself wanting to sit, like Father Abraham, at the entrance of my tent in the heat of the day, at rest, waiting, open, ready to welcome the three strange angels who I knew would surely appear.

I can feel the presence of both my mother and my father in me. I have an old photograph of myself at four-years-old that makes me laugh because it tells so much of who I am. A shy little girl stands facing the sun with a slight frown on her face, a hand shading her eyes. She is wearing a grass skirt that her father had just brought her from Hawaii and a long-sleeved flannel shirt. The grass skirt and the flannel shirt—there I am! The two sides of myself, my mother and my father reflected.

When I was almost five years old my mother told me we were moving from Scott to Swainsboro so that I could begin school. She asked if I would like to go to kindergarten. I felt that combination of fear and desire that often comes when one is asked to face something new, but I learned that desire can outweigh fear. I knew my answer was yes. I knew intuitively that my parents were my world, and I would be fine if I were with them. We moved into a little duplex apartment on Church Street. It was close enough to the school for me to look out my school room window and see *home*—a good place for a very shy little girl. The world was still cozy. I loved that apartment and still dream about it.

Soon after his return home from the war my father opened a small women's clothing shop. His new role was the other reason for our move to Swainsboro. The store, which opened before my brother's birth, became almost like the middle child in our family. We all loved it over the 50-plus years of its existence. When it first opened, no one could have imagined how that store would grow. My father was a good businessman and took pride in seeing his work develop into a prosperous undertaking. My mother, with her good taste in clothes, became an excellent buyer for the store. I spent many childhood hours there and loved looking at the pretty things and watching customers carefully choose what they wanted to buy.

World War II had just ended, and many of the salesmen who came with lines of ladies' clothes were Jews from Europe. After he introduced me to these men, my father would address me as if I were an adult and say, "I want you to know this man. He spent time in a concentration camp during the war and suffered more than you and I can imagine. We don't want to forget that." Then he would ask the man to show me the number tattooed on his arm. I hope *never* to forget that. The time after the war was tinged with the sadness of loss and the awareness of the horrors that humans are capable of, but the worst was over, at least for a while. There was, as well, a quiet happiness and hope for a better tomorrow.

My father invited a partner into the business, and the store continued to grow for years, becoming a small department store that held a full corner of the square in downtown Swainsboro. Small family-owned businesses thrived for several decades after the war. Big box stores began making inroads during the 1980s, and they were deadly to these small family-operated businesses. By the early 1990s the small stores were failing. Dolores and Woody's, opened in March of 1946, finally closed its doors at the end of 1998.

Chapter 2

Getting More Acquainted with Life

Unquestionably, the most exciting thing that happened after we moved to Swainsboro was the birth of my brother when I was almost six. It was January 12, 1948, when my grandmother took me to the hospital in Dublin to see my mother and to meet Denny. When I saw him I fell into a state of instant love and total fascination. I believe someone must have sent my mother hyacinths in celebration of the new baby, because to this day whenever I smell hyacinths my mind goes immediately to his birth.

I was nearly seven when I saw pain up close for the first time. Denny broke his leg. It was on the day he had taken his first short walk of four or five steps. At lunch he lifted the tray of his highchair and jumped out, breaking his thigh bone. His screaming would not stop. When he came home from the hospital he was in a cast from his waist to his heel on one leg and to his knee on the other leg. He was immobilized for weeks. My parents were sick with worry. My mother developed pleurisy, and my grandmothers took turns helping us through those hard weeks.

I was given my first experience of caring for others in a serious way. My desire to help took root. As a second grader I was asked to do my part. I felt a sense of responsibility and a growing confidence of my place in the household.

In school my fifth-grade teacher introduced me to a set of biographies for children, and I think I read every one of them. The stories of Clara Barton, founder of the Red Cross and Florence Nightingale, pioneer in nursing captivated me. I wrote reports on them and stood at the foot of my parents' bed speaking about these valiant women. The bed became a great crowd of people, and I was hoping to inspire them to do something good with their lives. I did this kind of thing as a younger child too, except at that point I was clearly preaching! I would upend a rectangular footstool, making it a pulpit, from which I could preach—always about God's love. I expect by fifth grade I was aware, though perhaps not consciously, that women did not preach, and so I moved from the pulpit to the lectern. (Many years later the footstool that was my pulpit would sit in front of my chair in the Anchorhold. One day after a session of spiritual direction in which I had talked with someone about God's tender, faithful love for each of us, it dawned on me that the 'pulpit' of my childhood now sat before me. I was preaching one-on-one.)

My growing up years were filled with wonderful friends. We had the best of times together, and I remember them with great fondness. I had a very active childhood and a good social life as a young person, yet underlying that was what I now would name as a preference for quiet. Love of solitude was writ in my cells. I remember the quiet of our living room, where I sat reading a biography of Joan of Arc with the sun falling on my back and shoulders. I knew what her 'voices' were like and I felt kinship with Joan, the young girl who knew how to sit quietly and listen and whose warrior spirit wanted to respond to life with all that was in her.

A Church-Shaped Child

In my early years, still newborn to this world, my eyes not yet fully open, I was given the gift of love. Nested in family I felt secure. The First Methodist Church of Swainsboro was like an extension of home, a safe place for a child, providing me with a wider family. The people loved me, and I loved them. They encouraged and nurtured me and helped teach me the rudiments of faith. They, indeed, "called me by name,"[1] giving me an early sense of who I was intended to be. They taught me that I belonged to them, and more importantly, I belonged to God. I was not left to the seductive voices of secular culture. This congregation gave me the voice of God. They gave me Christ. The love, the worship, the reverence that I saw and absorbed there, as well as in my home, provided strong spiritual formation. I was set on a firm foundation, one I could wish for every child.

Here among these people a flame of love was kindled in me, awakening a longing to be a part of Christ's compelling vision for the world. What I had yet to learn was that awakening was an ongoing, always-in-process happening.

As I grew my eyes opened, and I began to come into consciousness. The parameters of my childhood were shifting and broadening. In the next few years I would be introduced to people and ideas that would expand my thinking and way of looking at things. In time I grew beyond much of my early learning. I now have very different views from those shared by many of the people who are a part of that dear congregation. Yet the love endures. I believe love can undergird relationship even where ideological differences divide. Growing up in the Methodist Church, I was raised under the aegis of John Wesley: "Though we cannot think alike, may we not love alike? May we not be of one heart, though we are not of one opinion?"[2]

I was born with a naturally contemplative bent. This was nurtured throughout my childhood, and then as a young person God strengthened this gift in an unexpected way. I took piano lessons. After a few years, my music teacher, who was organist at the Methodist Church, introduced me to the organ. She soon had me playing for the night service a couple of times a month. This set me up for the formative experience of practicing almost daily in the church sanctuary. Each afternoon I would step into that beautiful space where shafts of light fell through stained-glass windows and holy silence breathed around and through me. I found the solitude bracing. As I played hymns over and over, the vibrant chords of the organ mingled with the quiet, stirring my depths. This atmosphere alone was enough to open my heart to the enveloping Presence. God drew me close.

I grew to love the hymns of the church—words and music, but I was not destined to be an outstanding musician. It seemed that was not the point of my being in that holy space. I believe the purpose of those long, solitary afternoons was to awaken me to deep relationship with God, to make me aware that the membrane between human and divine is thin and permeable. The silence—it was always the silence that moved me so. God was alive in it. God drew me there to speak tenderly to me, and my heart opened. I experienced the interpenetration of the human and divine. My life still holds the contours of its early shaping. My contemplative bent has held through years of testing. But there had to be some testing!

Getting more Acquainted with Life

Transplanted to a Bigger Pot

"Early on the first day of the week, while it was still dark...."³ These words, ever descriptive of life, seem poignantly appropriate for the 1940s and '50s, the years of my childhood. The culture of my growing up was homogeneous. Stability still held sway. Old institutions and familiar mores and mindsets were still intact. People saw life mostly through a narrow lens. An unimaginable dawn was on the way. A new world was at hand. Or more precisely, we were about to be given the opportunity to *see our world anew*. Big issues were on the horizon. Rising cultural tensions were calling for new vision. The milieu of my young adulthood would be very different from that of my childhood.

In the summer of 1959, following my junior year in high school, I attended the National Conference of Methodist Youth at Purdue University. The experience took me up and out of my small life, giving me a new definition of greatness. It opened my world, enlarged my vision, deepened my faith, stirred my heart. I got to hear Eleanor Roosevelt, one of the greatest women of her era, speak. To this day I feel honored to have been in her presence. Odetta, with her big, full voice, sang with the outcry of soul, introducing me to the early songs of the civil rights struggle. Dave Brubeck and his quartet played rich, creamy jazz. I heard Bach played on a mighty pipe organ and radical readings selected from J.D. Salinger's *Catcher in the Rye*. I was wide-eyed with wonder. This event set a large context for me to move in. It felt like being repotted. It gave me root-room. One week, and my concept of Church had expanded. And it kept on expanding.

My mind was being changed, my heart was being stirred. I went off to college, where a new world awaited me. These were my coming-of-age years, and we were on the edge of revolutionary change. An old world was passing, the night far spent—a new day was springing forth! The years at Emory-at-Oxford, "Big Emory," Duke Divinity School and the Ecumenical Institute set me in a new direction, turning my interest and energy outward, challenging me to read and think more broadly, developing my leadership skills, and linking my faith to action. Two life-changing books for me during my college days were James Baldwin's *The Fire Next Time* and John Howard Griffin's *Black Like Me*. I heard Martin Luther King, Jr. speak, and was moved to my core. Civil Rights and the Vietnam War were the great issues of the day, with the women's movement just emerging. Social justice became the driving force of my life, pushing me out of myself and into action on behalf of others. I wanted to be awake for this big, bold happening of my time. I felt the truth of Christopher Fry's wake-up call:

> Dark and cold we may be, but this
> Is no winter now. The frozen misery
> Of centuries breaks, cracks, begins to move;
> The thunder is the thunder of floes,
> The thaw, the flood, the upstart Spring.
> Thank God our time is now when wrong
> Comes up to face us everywhere,
> Never to leave us till we take
> The longest stride of soul men ever took.
> Affairs are now soul size.
> The enterprise
> Is exploration into God.[4]

Chapter 3

INTO THE WORLD

My first job after divinity school was with Wesley Foundation at Clemson University in South Carolina. Richard Elliott, who was Director of Wesley Foundation, wrote to ask me if I would be interested in the position of Associate Director. Someone at Duke had given him my name. When I went for a job interview he met me at the bus stop, and right away he was teasing me, putting me at ease, talking politics, voicing his feelings about Civil Rights and the Vietnam War. He was young and good-looking, passionate about his work with the students and protesting the constraints of a very conservative time and place. I felt I had found a kindred spirit. He told me about visiting the Ecumenical Institute, a Christian community in Chicago, and his interest in our going there for a summer program as a way of beginning our work together. I had read of the Institute and had heard its founder Joe Mathews speak, so I was very excited about spending a summer in that community on the West Side of Chicago. By the end of the interview I had given an unequivocal "Yes!" to my first full-time job. I was promised a yearly salary of $5,000 and felt absurdly rich.

Soon after I arrived in Clemson, I had a call from a woman in town asking me for a punch recipe for a party. I was surprised at such a request until I heard her ask, "Well, aren't you the social director?" It was 1966, and such was the world of women. The job at Clemson did not last long. A year after my arrival Richard needed to move, and I was left with a new Director. It turned out that the new Director and I were less than compatible. As Associate I was in a vulnerable position.

Wesley Foundation sponsored a tutoring program for black children in a nearby town, making us unpopular with the larger community. We also were engaged in voter registration in the surrounding area. Some students from the University of South Carolina came over about one weekend a month to help us with this project. Among these students was the first black student to attend USC. She spent Friday nights with me and worked all day Saturday; then she and the other students returned to Columbia. It was exciting to be a part of this freedom struggle in some small way. Martin Luther King, Jr.'s powerful oratory; his presentation of his dream straight from the lips of the Old Testament prophets; his message of God's boundless, unrelenting love and God's desire for all people to live in freedom—this vision was worth embracing, a vision worth committing myself to. This work, along with my anti-war stance, brought an end to my time in Clemson.

The conflict in Vietnam was troubling. What was the purpose of all that killing? People were beginning to question the U.S. involvement there, an involvement about to become a hot-button issue that eventually would divide our nation, separating regions, classes, political parties, communities, generations, families—and the church. I was opposed to the Vietnam War, an unacceptable position in most of the country, most certainly in the South, in 1966-67. I was participating in anti-war marches, and a very small group of us at Clemson were handing out anti-war material on campus each week. The tension in the air made me know that my time at Clemson was coming to an end. The Wesley Foundation students asked me not to resign, so I decided to stay the course and see what might happen.

The University banned me from the campus. The Civil Rights work and anti-war protests we were engaged in drew a lot of heat. Twice I was followed part-way home at night after leaving a Civil Rights gathering, tailed by a driver with bright lights on. And almost daily I was receiving anonymous phone calls and threats to do me harm. If someone else answered my telephone, I was asked for by name. I was hurt, angry and afraid. God had called me to take my deeply held beliefs into the public sphere, and now I was learning firsthand that when you take a public stance on your beliefs you must not be surprised at retaliation.

One night after a threatening phone call had left me feeling vulnerable and unnerved, someone knocked on my door. Though trembling with fear, I knew I had to face whoever was there. I took a deep breath and opened the door. My downstairs neighbor was standing before me with an enormous bouquet of yellow daffodils he had picked for me that afternoon. He came in and helped me settle down and regain my composure. On that night, with daffodils lighting up the room, I read aloud the ending lines of a D.H. Lawrence poem I loved:

> What is the knocking?
> What is the knocking at the door in the night?
> It is somebody wants to do us harm.
> No, no, it is the three strange angels.
> Admit them, admit them.[1]

When I saw that I was going to be fired, I called my parents to ask if I could stay with them until I could get redirected. My father wrote me a letter saying "If you believe in this enough to fight for it, then fight. But keep your gloves high in the air, no punches below the belt. We believe in you." The issues I was involved in split families. I knew young people whose parents had rejected them. I had no fear of that. The love and support of my family were invaluable.

In November of 1967 the Board of Higher Education of the South Carolina Conference of the Methodist Church met in Columbia to decide what to do with me. I was put up for the day at a hotel there and asked to stay in my room so that I would be available for questioning. I spent a long day in the hotel room. I was asked no questions. In the late afternoon someone came to pick me up. There had been a heated meeting, and I had been fired. I left Clemson almost a year and a half after I had arrived there.

I returned to Swainsboro with the bitter taste of humiliation in my mouth. Young, unseasoned and angry, I could not get my bearings. Things had not turned out the way I had expected. My plans had been thwarted. Resistance was my first response—and it was strong and recurrent. I needed time. As I wrestled with my failure I began to see that far from being the end, it actually led to my freedom.

I was learning a prime lesson of the spiritual journey: One has to be broken to be opened. This insight was a basic lesson in humility. God is not present to serve me, to prop up my ideas of where I need to work and what I need to do. Life is about serving the One who sent me. I lost my naivete about the church, about other institutions, and most importantly, about myself. I could sense that my life was badly out of balance. I had become so engaged in social action that I had neglected the contemplative part of myself.

Life is risk and challenge, full of storms and struggles. Life is beauty, blue skies, gentleness and joy. Life and death, light and darkness, joy and sorrow—the givens of life. That is reality. The time had come to open my arms to what Zorba the Greek called "the full catastrophe." God was summoning me to receive with love and gratitude the full gift of life. It was time for me to learn that if I stretched out my inadequate arms to encircle it *all* in love, I would find that I was compassed by Christ who would enable me to do the impossible. Life is good! God pronounces it so, and blesses it by becoming one of us, sharing our every load. God needs this very life of mine. I am a human being, and that is what I am meant to be—a particular person with particular gifts in a particular time and place. God's intention for me is that I live *my* life, and that I live it as one who is *sent from Beyond*—sent with purpose.

The big question: Would I accept the gift of my life? When I was still and quiet enough I was aware of the *beyond* overlapping my present life, making itself felt, revealing a sense of purpose. In the silence I could hear the Mystery questioning, "Will you co-create with me? Yes or No?" I knew that only my Yes would allow purpose to unfold. My task was to accept the risk of working out my purpose, and with every failure, to willingly begin anew, again and again. What would my answer be?

Through the months of love and care given me by my family I began to heal. At last I was both strong enough and weak enough to answer. I wanted to say yes to God's call. I wanted to say yes to God each day.

Chapter 4

Next Steps

I needed a break from church as I healed. I left Clemson exhausted and sick with a deep, resistant bronchial infection that lasted for months. Looking back I can see God's hand clearly at work. My mother gave me tender care, and I slowly recovered. I signed a contract to teach a Title-1 kindergarten class January-May of 1968. The day after I signed the contract I had a call from a man at Atlanta University asking if I could be the "Girl Friday" for Maynard Jackson's south Georgia Senate campaign. The man who called had been trying to find me for several days, but had been looking in Statesboro rather than Swainsboro. I believe that God's hand covered me then and redirected my life. I almost surely would have said yes to a political future if I had not just signed a contract to teach. Then, in the summer of 1968 I worked with Head Start, in charge of social work for the county. We integrated doctors' offices and other helping venues in Swainsboro and Emanuel County.

I moved to Atlanta at the end of the summer, went to the DeKalb County Board of Education Office and said I would like to teach in a black school. They took one look at my white face and asked, "Which one?" I chose Victoria Simmons Elementary, a small school in Stone Mountain. I loved teaching there that year, however, in order to integrate the school system, it was closed at the end of the year. The black children would henceforth attend the nearby "white school." The principal asked me to lead three afternoon workshops for the teachers from both schools to help prepare them for integration—a challenge I was honored to undertake. We dedicated the workshops to Rosa Parks. And I knew the time had come for me to move on.

In September 1969 I went to Pendle Hill, a Quaker study center just outside Philadelphia. I was attracted there by an advertisement for a course in Gandhian philosophy and non-violent direct action. Outcroppings of violence in the peace movement had begun to disturb me. When I got to Pendle Hill I was surprised to find that, although the ad for the course in non-violent direct action had gotten my attention, I was there for something else. I needed the silence and contemplative atmosphere of that Quaker community. I reconnected with a part of myself that had been lost in the years of social action. As a child I had loved quiet and solitude, reading, listening, watching—things I had not honored for a long time. The move outward was important, but I had gone far enough. The outer life is only a part of the whole. It was time to turn inward again, toward the Spirit present there, ready to guide if listened to. Quaker Douglas Steere says that activism and overwork are contemporary forms of violence. It is easy to lose one's balance. I began to pray again. I laid the tip of my finger against the stillness, remembering it from long ago. It whispered to me, and I trusted it against all odds. "Be still," the voice said.

A Particle of Light

Church Work

After my time at Pendle Hill my mother said she could feel a deep change in me—something truer to myself, a quietness, a stillness, a steadiness. I took a job at Inner City United Methodist Church in Savannah. It was the perfect way for me to "reenter the fold." I worked with Sammy Clark, an old friend who was a shining light for a lot of young United Methodists in the 1960s and '70s. My two years there gave me time to test the waters of church for myself. Would I, could I…should I work in the institutional church? I was far from certain about that, and I was miserable in my uncertainty.

One Sunday afternoon I sat crying in my apartment. I began looking through a stack of papers from my time at the Ecumenical Institute in Chicago in the summer of 1966. I came upon a paper by H. Richard Niebuhr entitled, "The Nature and Existence of God," and I began reading. As I became engrossed in the paper my tears stopped. I heard a knock at the door, and two men from the Ecumenical Institute were standing on the stoop of my tiny apartment. I had not been in touch with them for a long time, and then there they were! As we visited I felt a desire awaken in me. What about the possibility of living in that community? On that May afternoon I told them that I wanted to become an intern at the Atlanta House beginning in September. Once again I was drawn on.

I lived for a year in the Atlanta House of the Ecumenical Institute. The Institute, founded by Joseph Mathews was a venture in community life, based on the old monastic orders of the Church. It was an exciting experiment in life together, interpreting old models for a new age—mixing men, women, solitaries and families, lay and clergy. We lived as a religious community, rising at 4:30 a.m. to pray the Morning Office together and then to discuss whatever article or book we were studying. Our morning and evening meals were eaten together. Each person had an outside job, and after breakfast we headed out for a day of work. I worked for a cardiologist at Emory Hospital. Our salaries were put into a common account, and we were given a small monthly stipend to cover personal expenses. We returned to the House in the late afternoon to tend to the needs of community life. On weekends we taught courses on religious studies. Many people went through RS-1, the basic religious studies course we offered, and many lives were changed by that experience. On Sunday evenings we had our Common Meal, gathered around the big dining room table. It was our Eucharistic celebration for the week. I liked the challenge and order of the Institute. I needed the call to audacity that it issued, and I needed (for a future day) the particular formation in community life that it gave. After a year at the Atlanta House I knew it was time to try to make peace more fully with the church, to be a part of an ordinary local church again.

I took a job with First United Methodist Church in Brunswick as Director of Christian Education. Within months I knew I was not to stay there for long. What was the meaning of these short-term stays here and there? In all this tumbling onward, job by job, place by place, experience by experience, I was beginning to understand that each part of the journey was important. I could see that what I learned in one way station prepared me for the next. If I gave myself to what was set before me, if I were attentive and open to the present moment I would be made ready for the next step, given the gifts I would need for the next task.

During my third year the church sent me to Bolivia for three months to help a missionary couple. I was to speak to women's groups and help train Vacation Bible School teachers. I also wanted to learn some Spanish. The unexpected happened.

A Particle of Light

An Unexpected Grace

Early in my time in Bolivia a baby girl was found abandoned in a ditch. A couple walking by heard her crying. She was covered with dust. The woman stayed with her, and the man went into town to get the social service worker. The social worker, whom I had met earlier, phoned one of the missionaries I was working with and asked if she thought I might take the child. For some reason she was sure that this infant was to be my baby. Abandoned babies, often malnourished or sick, were not uncommon in the area. This beautiful little girl, however, was perfect.

After half an hour of considering what I might be getting into, I said YES. I had been so abundantly loved as a child, I could never have said no and continued to live with myself. I went to the social service office, a big room with a desk, some folding chairs along the walls, and a single light bulb hanging from a long cord in the middle of the ceiling. After my eyes adjusted to the dim light I saw the baby. She was lying naked on the bare wood floor. The binding strip the mother used to support her baby's back was lying next to her—the only link she had to a vanished life. It was truly love at first sight. I looked at her, and I loved her. I picked her up, held her, took her to my room and cared for her.

I prepared a little bed for her by putting a pillow in a dresser drawer and made diapers out of sugar sacks. I met the milk man each morning to get a pitcher full of milk which I then scalded to make it safe for drinking. And I took her into my heart. She had been carried on the back of her mother, so her spine was very straight, which made holding her in my arms a bit awkward. However, over the course of a week I could feel her body begin to change, being reshaped to fit comfortably into the crook of my arm and to feel at rest against my shoulder.

She was a parable of God's love. I became aware of how love reshapes us, and I understood how God could look at us and love us, and long for the very best for us. I knew a little of how God felt when he looked at each creature and said, "Very good." And I knew that the love I felt for her was only a shadow of the love God feels for us: love beyond imagining.

I took the baby to a hospital in Santa Cruz to find out how old she might be. After some simple tests I was told she was about two months old and that I should give her a birthdate, which I did. Having fallen in love with this child I knew I wanted to bring her back to the States with me. I met with committees at several levels of the Bolivian government trying to get approval. In the end my request was denied. I was told to bring her in so she could be placed in an orphanage. I could hardly bear that thought and asked if they would allow me to look for a family to take her instead. They agreed, and I had one day to find someone.

I had met a Mennonite couple who had no children and were considering adopting. The woman helping me through this process took me to talk with them. I asked if they would take the child. After a brief discussion they said yes. They were in Bolivia with Mennonite Central Committee and would be there for a couple of years—long enough to work through the red tape of adopting the child. In time, they brought her to the States where she became a naturalized citizen. And they gave me the sweet blessing of staying in touch with me.

Throughout her childhood they told her of my part in her story, and in 1991, when she was about to turn sixteen, she asked to meet me. Our reunion was beautiful. I had last seen her in 1975 when she was three-months-old. We met again as if we had never been apart. She wanted to hear me tell the part of her story that I knew, and it was my privilege to share with her those long-ago memories of seeing her for the first time, of picking her up from the floor and holding her close in my arms, of falling in love with her and wanting all that was best for her. I had one photograph to give her, a picture of me holding a beautiful baby with a shock of dark hair and big dark eyes. She seemed to be holding me in return. She has visited me several times. So I have had an ongoing relationship with this beautiful woman, now a nurse and a mother with children of her own. Jessica.

This experience shaped me, melted and molded me. The moment I picked up that tiny baby was a moment of pure grace. God had put into my arms an abandoned child, a baby found in a ditch. I looked at her tiny face and into her dark brown eyes, the depth of which I could not begin to fathom. I held her close and raised her to my cheek burying my face in hers. Never again could I hold the poverty of the world at a distance. It was in my arms. The poverty of a baby abandoned on a rural dirt road in eastern Bolivia! Bolivia is one of the poorest countries in the Americas. Life had all but let this child down, had left her helpless with no more than her breath and her cry—but with the innate hope and will to live. I held that vulnerability in my arms—and I knew the sorrow of it.

What better way could God have placed in my heart the understanding of the power and gift of human community—our utter dependence on one another. Looking at this tender child opened my eyes and heart. The mystery of this meeting, the gratitude, the sense of love and responsibility still overwhelms me. It is such a privilege to have been a part of her story. It has taught me about the particularity and the immensity of love. It has opened a well of wonder in me. How is it that this child lying in the dust of a ditch cried out at just the right time to be heard by another human? How is it that a couple walking the lonely road happened by at just the right time to hear her? How is it that, connection by connection, her life and my life were linked? I know not. But I wonder.

I returned to the United States broken-hearted at having to leave her. I could not understand. I could only surrender. I began praying with the barren Rachel of Israel, as she cried out in longing, "Give me children lest I die."[1] That was to be answered in a way I could not have imagined.

I came back to Brunswick to continue my life and work there for a while. But I knew the door to that part of my life was closing, and as it closed so did the door to my working within the United Methodist Church. Longing for guidance, I prayed that God would take my life and use it fully. I was ready to go wherever God wanted to lead me. Guidance was given.

Chapter 5

I Will Lead You Home

On Monday, June 20, 1977 I met Sr. Peter Claver, the dear Hannah. It happened like this: I had been in Brunswick for three and a half years and knew that it was time for me to take the next step along the way. I did not know what I was to do, so I began praying seriously about that. William Temple, former Archbishop of Canterbury, said of intercessory prayer: "When I pray coincidences happen, when I don't, they do not." I think this can be said of prayer in general, when we pray coincidences happen—a book, an opportunity, a person shows up at the right time. If we truly seek we will find—and not by chance. A deep interest in spiritual life was beginning to flower in me. As I read and re-read some of the spiritual classics—*The Cloud of Unknowing*, Jean-Pierre de Caussade's *Abandonment to Divine Providence*, Evelyn Underhill's book *Mysticism*, Thomas Kelly's *A Testament of Devotion* and Thomas Merton's *New Seeds of Contemplation*—I began praying more deeply and in ways new to me. I was hungering and thirsting for God. *The Liturgy of the Hours* (the Divine Office) fell into my hands and became my daily companion. I became re-acquainted with the

Psalms, reading them as if for the first time. I longed for guidance and could find no one with whom to talk. And an image kept recurring, a house, where I was often sweeping the porch.

Along with the image came a desire, to open a house of some sort. I talked to a few people in the United Methodist Church in south Georgia about this. Responses ranged from kind shrugs to blank looks. Nothing developed. I think that was in part because I did not yet have enough clarity. The vision was embryonic, not yet fully formed. And I also think that the United Methodist Church simply did not have the imagination to help me. My family offered to help me find a house. I saw one in Swainsboro that looked a lot like the house in my head. My father checked it out, but it had been condemned by the city and was about to be torn down. I had to let that go. Looking back I can see that I was being pushed to the outer edge of the Church that had reared me and which I loved deeply. I did not know where to turn. Sometimes I wonder what would have happened to me if God had not pointed me toward the Catholic Church. I did not yet know that sometimes when a person is seeking to love God with heart, soul, mind and strength, yet cannot find help from others, the Holy Spirit intervenes with direct guidance. I would soon learn that essential divine knowledge.

This period was a crisis time for me. I knew the time had come to take another step, but I had no sense of direction, only the strong sense that I must go. As an act of faith I decided to give up my job and wait.

Dorothy Day had long been one of my heroines. She had begun the Catholic Worker movement in the 1930s and lived among the poor in New York. Through the Brunswick library I was able to get a copy of her then out-of-print autobiography, *The Long Loneliness*. I took the old falling-apart copy to my apartment and began to read. In the book she told the story of how Peter Maurin, a French peasant, mysteriously showed up on her doorstep one day, and it was he who helped her get her philosophy straight, get the Catholic Worker movement started, and the houses of hospitality for the poor established. As I read about Peter Maurin I began to pray, "God, who will be my Peter Maurin?"

A couple of days after I finished the book I received a letter from my divinity school roommate and dear friend, Betty Hanigan, who lived in Erie, Pennsylvania. In the letter she said, "Go to Rome, Georgia, and meet Sr. Peter Claver who has recently moved there from Erie. She has a small House of Prayer and is lonely for companionship." Needless to say, I was astounded—someone named Peter whom I should go and visit. I had never been to Rome, but next day I got in my car and set out. I did not call ahead. I found the house and knocked on the door. An old woman appeared. She was 78 at the time. I remember standing there thinking, "Dear God, what kind of a trick are you playing on me?" But she invited me in, and we sat at her dining room table and talked. As it turned out, we had read many of the same books, had many of the same interests, and she was a personal friend of Dorothy Day. After we had talked for a while she said she felt this was a providential meeting. She encouraged me, saying "You must do something creative with your life." Then, "People say you need money to do things, but I don't wait for money. I've never gone lacking." This was the good bread I had been searching for, the refreshing water for the desert of my heart. Sweet relief. I, too, was certain that it was the kind, loving hand of Providence that had brought me there. She asked if I would like to come to live and work with her. I said yes to her invitation, and we reached our hands across a barrier—a young Methodist woman living and working with an old Roman Catholic Sister. Such a thing was not ordinarily done in those days.

I Will Lead You Home

I returned to south Georgia to tell people that I was moving to Rome to live in a House of Prayer with a Catholic sister. When they heard the words 'house of prayer' many people seemed to think I was going off to read palms. And when they heard the word 'Catholic' they thought I was headed for Rome, Italy.

In that in-between moment when I stood on the threshold of a new life, I spent a night on Jekyll Island. On a Sunday evening I sat alone on the beach, the water shimmering in the dusky light. There beside that mighty, mysterious old womb of life, with the sound of the ocean as background music I prayed the Sunday Evening Office. A line from Psalm 110 enthralled me: "From the womb before the dawn I begot you."[1] I stayed with it. "From the womb *before the dawn* I begot you." "From the womb before the dawn *I begot* you." "From the womb before the dawn I begot *you*." I stopped right there. God has been laboring from the beginning to bring each of us forth…and I understood that profound message that evening. I understood it personally. God continues to labor in us and for us, so that we can come into the fullness of who we are meant to be. Whatever questions and fears I held about the future fell away. I was ready to move ahead. My path curved toward a still far-distant Green Bough that night.

I moved into the House of Prayer in Rome on September 8, 1977, Feast of the Birth of Mary. I felt that I had come home, and I was sure that I was to start some kind of House of Prayer. It would take a while.

Chapter 6

Sojourner in the Land of Learning

Hannah Fahy (who would later take the name Peter Claver) was born in Rome, Georgia, into a prominent family. Her mother was Jewish, but she had embraced Catholicism when she was a young woman. Her father, an Irishman, established a successful clothing business to support his family of eleven children. Hannah was one of four girls, none of whom married. All of the children were well-educated and several excelled in their particular fields. After high school Hannah left Rome for New York to pursue a career in ballet, but her family insisted that she go to college. After graduating from Trinity College in Washington, D.C., she experienced a call to religious life and in the mid-1920s entered the Missionary Servants of the Most Blessed Trinity, an order founded to serve the poor in the rural South. Hannah had seen the suffering of black people and felt called to address the wrongs she had witnessed. When she became a Trinitarian she took the name of Peter Claver, a Jesuit of the 1600s, who devoted his life to caring for slaves who were being shipped from Africa to the Americas. Sr. Peter Claver, throughout her life worked with African-Americans, poor whites, women and prisoners. As a young sister working in New York she met Dorothy Day. It was Sr. Peter Claver who gave Dorothy the first dollar for the beginning of the Catholic Worker—a dollar received from a collection at a street corner mission. The two became friends. Later in the 1970s Sr. Peter helped start a House of Prayer in Erie, Pennsylvania. During this time she also became interested in Jean Vanier's work of establishing communities in France for people with intellectual disabilities. He called his venture L'Arche. Sr. Peter encouraged the founding of a L'Arche community in Erie—the first in the United States. In 1976 she returned to Rome, her hometown, to open a House of Prayer there. Over the years Sr. Peter became well-known in Catholic circles, receiving several prestigious awards late in her life. I had the privilege of being her close friend.

Sister Peter Claver (I called her by her given name, Hannah) and I lived together for over a year. We prayed the Daily Office morning and evening, followed by an hour of silence in our chapel. After supper I read aloud for us, and then we prayed Compline. We spent a lot of time in silence, read a lot and offered weekly Scripture reflection groups for people who wanted to come. Our life together was good. She recognized and confirmed who I was at the core of my being, and she encouraged me without hesitation. In some strange way I think she had been waiting for me, ready to train another to carry the work of prayer, ready to pass on the wisdom garnered over a lifetime. We remained close friends until she died in 2004 at the age of 105. I still feel her presence and prayer undergirding me.

Hannah was interested in "doing something for the women of Rome," and I was too. At a meeting of Church Women United she presented the idea of beginning a shelter for women and their children. We invited any people who were interested to meet with us at the House of

Prayer, starting in January, 1978. A small ecumenical group of women and a few men began meeting with us. After several months we knew that this idea could become a reality. We were already calling the shelter Hospitality House.

One day Margaret Whitworth, who was an active part of the group, told me that if I would become director of the shelter she felt we could get it up and running. I said I would need time to consider this suggestion. I had moved to Rome to be at the House of Prayer and *knew* that I was to start a House of Prayer of my own. I talked the matter over with Hannah. She did not want me to leave. "You are a contemplative, and you don't need to take on the work of being director," she said. We knew, however, that the shelter needed to open. So I said, "I'll go for six months and get it started and then come back to the House of Prayer." I left the House of Prayer with a heavy heart. I found the work at the shelter rich and challenging—and was surprised by a growing sense that it was somehow necessary for my development. Within a couple of months Hannah became sick and early in 1979 was moved back to her mother house in Philadelphia. Her House of Prayer in Rome closed.

Soon after I moved to Rome, Steve Bullington contacted me. Steve's parents, Margaret and Elick, and my parents were friends by way of Methodist connections. Elick, a United Methodist minister, served for five years as pastor of First United Methodist Church in Swainsboro, during which time our families grew close. Steve's spiritual journey eventually led him toward seminary.

When I moved to Rome, Steve was a student at Candler School of Theology at Emory University. He heard by way of a mutual friend that I was living at a House of Prayer with a Catholic Sister. As someone already well-formed in prayer, he was very interested in my life there and called to ask if he could visit me. He came for a visit in late 1977, and so began a blessed relationship with a very dear man. He continued to come back several times each year while I was in Rome. This life of prayer made sense to him. Every time Steve came to visit he and I would pray together. I introduced him to the Divine Office, and he began praying it. Through the shelter years when he came we always had Holy Communion together, sometimes just the two of us, and sometimes joined by people from the shelter or community. One of my favorite services of the whole year is the Wesley Covenant Service prayed on New Year's Day. I asked Steve to come and lead it for us. Nearly every year while I was at the shelter he came for New Year's celebration. I told him of my intention to start a House of Prayer at some point. He expressed interest in being a part of that. I could not imagine how and when it would happen, but I had a profound sense of knowing that it would.

I left Hospitality House in the autumn of 1986. I stayed there for eight years, all the while keeping in my heart the calling to start a House of Prayer. These were the years; this was the setting where my in-depth training would take place.

Chapter 7

The Story of Hospitality House

I went to Rome to live at the House of Prayer, but Hospitality House seemed bound to happen. Once Sr. Peter Claver planted the idea at a meeting of Church Women United the seed began to take root. Interest grew. People came from all around Rome to help—women, men, young and old, people of different religious backgrounds, different races and classes and political opinions—all came together around this vision of a shelter for women and their children. Hospitality House was the second shelter for women in the state of Georgia, opening several months after the Marietta shelter and a few weeks before the Atlanta shelter. We had no maps to go by, no operating instructions, and few models. We all pulled together, let our imaginations be at play, and poured ourselves into the work.

Mary Swinford was our first Board Chair. I was founding Director. At our first Board meeting we made a big decision: we would operate on faith and would receive no government funding. I would receive a stipend of $200 a month, plus health insurance. I gave a brief talk, ending with a couplet from Goethe:

> Whatever you can do or dream you can, begin it,
> Boldness has genius, power, and magic in it.

These lines, like a match to tinder, set afire an adventurous spirit among us, stirring desire, vision and a willingness to work.

Hospitality House was a community ministry, composed mostly of volunteers. We were open to all kinds of ways Hospitality House could be of service to the community. Over the years we met, dreamed and brainstormed together, prayed together, partied together, agreed together, disagreed together. We worked together and depended mightily on one another. And we did it all rather well!

A $5,000 grant, from a United Methodist Women's National Assembly Offering and several generous gifts from local people enabled us to get started. We found an affordable house at 216 South Broad Street, in what was considered a rough neighborhood. Within ten days we had bought it. This decision was a venture of faith.

Hard work and brazen requests characterized our little group. I sometimes had a hard time asking people for help. One of our Board members quickly pegged my weakness and wrote me a note saying, "People are good and will help in whatever way they can. All they need is to be ASKED. Just remember, it never hurts to ask anybody for anything. The only thing that can happen is your feelings might get hurt. And we can rise above that." Sage advice that has served me well to this day.

Our dependence on volunteers created a bridge that spanned the gap between the shelter and the greater Rome community. Working at Hospitality House gave many a white woman her first opportunity to hold a black child and many a wealthy woman a chance to see and touch the face of poverty for the first time. It also gave opportunity for women and children who stayed at the shelter to feel the generosity and love of many people who were in a position to give time, money and support.

I moved into the shelter on Sunday, October 29, 1978. That afternoon we had an Open House. On the sidewalk in front of Hospitality House someone had written a message in chalk, "I have NO one." Those poignant words seemed to me the imperative for Hospitality House. We were to be the someone for those who had no one. Everyone who came that day stepped over that message.

No guests came during the first week. I was alone at the shelter and felt a clear need for help. I began to pray for another resident to come to help me. On Sunday, November 5, we had a second Open House. Near the end of the afternoon a beautiful young woman came in, a student in the School of Social Work at University of Georgia interning at the Mental Health Center in Rome. She just walked in and asked if it would be possible for her to come and live at the shelter with me. She wanted the experience as a part of her field training. She was a God-send. She moved in on Thursday and was the first of several young college students who worked with me over the years.

The location of the shelter made it impossible for us to remain hidden. So we hung out our shingle and became acquainted with our neighbors. Several prostitutes lived in the very active house next door. One night a few months after moving to South Broad I awoke to the flashing

The Story of Hospitality House

blue lights of 8 or 10 police cars—no sirens. That house was being raided. Everyone soon knew where Hospitality House was. The police were willing to come to our aid. Our neighbors became our friends, and we probably were as safe as we would have been in an unknown location.

Soon after moving to South Broad I began meeting the children of the neighborhood. As the months passed I got to know many of them. When the summer heat arrived, I could hear them outside my raised bedroom window. They were up late at night smoking cigarettes and plotting the next day's mischief. In 1979 we started a children's group called Hospitality Club. The group met weekly under the guidance of several dedicated supervisors. It grew and grew over the years. As I think of those children, now grown up, I wonder about them—where they are, how they are, if they have survived some difficult odds. What happens to our children who live in fear and want?

Within two years we were expanding. In January of 1980, we were offered a piece of property with an old house on it, three doors down from us. We had become aware that short term emergency shelter was not enough for many women. This new property became the opportunity to provide longer term care. We had not paid off the first house, however. How could we possibly think of taking on another? One of our Board members contacted the Garden Lakes Company, and someone from that development and construction business came to a Board meeting. He suggested that we tear down the old house and build a new one on the lot we had been given. How could we? Hope surged when the head of the Company became interested in the project, and Garden Lakes pledged to oversee the new building, providing the labor and most of the material. They brought us a key to the dried-in structure on

A Particle of Light

Christmas Eve, 1980. Several months later we were ready to open Hope House, a lovely place where women and their children could stay for up to three months.

Fran Shaw became Chair of our Board in 1980 and led us through this time, spending countless hours coordinating this burst of growth. Hospitality House, in those early years, pulsed with good energy. As we lived among the poor, and worked with the women and children who came to us, new needs became evident and new responses were called for. Hunger and lack of affordable housing for the poor were two big problems. We felt a responsibility to address those needs. We started Koinonia Kitchen, a soup kitchen that provided meals for the hungry. This project, under the leadership of Rena and Harold Story, grew into a major service to the Rome community. As a way to address housing needs, we established a chapter of Habitat for Humanity in Rome.

We also began a group called the Task Force, which could respond to particular needs of individuals in the community. We sponsored a week-long Vacation Bible School each summer for neighborhood and shelter children. We also offered a monthly gathering and meal for alumni of the House and neighborhood women and children. Once a week we offered Evening Prayer for any who wanted to come. All this, along with the weekly children's group that continued to meet, kept us spinning.

In 1984 Cornelia Gamble became Chair of the Board, overseeing the work of this busy period. As staff and activities grew, the house at 216 became too crowded. Those of us who lived there lived in a fishbowl.

We rented an apartment two doors away for staff and for retreat space. A few months later we bought an old house located between

The Story of Hospitality House

Hospitality and Hope. We named it Mary and Martha's and used the space for prayer, gatherings, staff housing, and community projects. We furnished the kitchen with a fine oven and worked with several women to form a small bread-baking group that we called Peace Goods. These women baked weekly and sold loaves of their homemade bread. It gave them a little spending money, and a tenth of what was earned went to local peace and justice work, like Koinonia Kitchen or Habitat for Humanity.

Hospitality House was a good mother, birthing and nurturing many offspring. I was privileged to be a part of all that imagination, creativity, and generosity. I left this beloved place in 1986, leaving Mark Manis as Chair of the Board through a time of transition. In 2008 I was asked to speak at the 30th anniversary of Hospitality House. My heart brimmed with gratitude for my years there. It is a very different place now but continues to serve women and their children who are seeking shelter from abusive relationships. I continue to pray for all who experience violence in their homes.

Chapter 8

Lessons from the Best of Teachers: Hospitality House Stories

Reflecting on my past I am aware that I had a lot to learn when I arrived at Hospitality House—a lot to learn before I would be ready to start a House of Prayer. My teachers were superb! They taught me well. People written on the margins of the world's pages are written in the very palm of God's hand.

The women and children who stayed with us at Hospitality House were my teachers, as were our neighbors, and those gracious and generous people who worked with me, who gave time, money and love. I have a deep devotion to the people of those years. It was a high privilege to live in the shelter—shoulder to shoulder, heart to heart—with so many courageous women and children.

"I think, dear child, the trouble and the long loneliness you hear me speak of is not far from me, which whensoever it is, happy success will follow. The pain is great, but very endurable, because He who lays on the burden also carries it." Before I ever moved to Rome I came upon this quote in Dorothy Day's book *The Long Loneliness*. The words are Mary Ward's, a 16th-17th century English nun. As I moved into Hospitality House, stepping over the words, "I have NO one," it seemed clear to me that I was there to be available, whatever that meant. And I was almost certain it meant that loneliness would be upon me and that there would be help in carrying it.

Not too long after moving into Hospitality House I had a reassuring dream: Two butterflies came to rest on me, a brilliant blue one on my shoulder, a white one on my head. I said again and again, "Thank you, God." On awaking I felt that the blue butterfly signified the devotion of my heart and the white one the blessing of Heaven. It seemed to me a dream of empowerment, as if I had been tapped with the sword of the Spirit, an accolade signifying the blessing of heart and head. I had a clear sense of *not being alone*. I had been made ready for my work at the shelter.

I was clear that my work was to BUILD UP and BE WITH the women and children God brought to me. That meant *meeting* each one with acceptance, *seeing* the dignity of each one and *listening* to the heart-cry of each. It also meant encouraging each person to reach for a higher quality of life. I was not there to 'do for' the women, but to support them with love, prayer and presence as they found their way. My deep desire was to learn to see Christ in my neighbor and to be Christ for my neighbor. This happens, of course, only by grace. My part was to practice living *as if*—which meant doing my best to be respectful and responsible in my daily life. Once in a while the gift I desired was given. Perhaps the greater gift of that time was learning to look full in the face of my own poverty and willfulness. I think of those times when I sat unmoved by the hardship of another's life and forgetful of the truth that "The lines have fallen for me in pleasant places."[1] Grace, thankfully, kept calling me to awareness and vigilance. Just as effort responds to grace, grace responds to effort. Now and again I knew full well Christ's presence.

I could never have lived this life without the strong support of a series of college students, a string of pearls, who lived and worked alongside me. And then there was the corps of great-hearted volunteers who helped staff the shelter. These were the people who made Hospitality House possible. I was there as learner. My part was to be open to receive all that God wanted to give me through them and through the women and children who stayed at the shelter. Though I did not know it until years later, I was being prepared for the work of beginning a House of Prayer.

As I look back I can see how my time at Hospitality House was vital training for the growth of my spiritual life. I was being taught to love—both by seeing how others love and by being placed in situations where I had to act boldly on behalf of others. Indeed I had entered "The School of Life, Love and the Long Haul." It was a boot camp of tears, laughter and stick-to-it-ness. I was being schooled day by day in *attentiveness*, *openness*, *caring* and *discipline*—the necessities for spiritual growth. Lesson One was, is and ever shall be: Practice. You learn by walking, falling down, getting up, walking, falling down, getting up.

The Way it is

Women do not have a corner on the market of hurt. Yet when compared to men, women have not had equal opportunity, help and concern about their welfare. A long history of patriarchal rule in Church, State and Culture has resulted in a peculiar and complicated powerlessness for women. Most of the women who came to Hospitality House were trying to leave abusive relationships. They would often come early in the week, following a weekend of abuse at the hands of an angry, and often drunk, husband.

Statistics show that up to 50 percent of the marriages in our society have some physical violence. This includes a push or slap. Ten percent have expressions of brutal violence: beating, cutting, burning, torturing—as well as mental and emotional abuse. Within my first month at the shelter we had a woman stay with us whose husband had branded his initials on her abdomen and another (who came to us from the hospital) whose husband had poured gasoline on her and set her afire. Both of these women eventually returned to those abusive relationships—one because her pastor insisted that divorce is a sin and under no circumstances can the marriage vows be broken; the other because she was unable to make a life for herself and her children alone.

It is easy to be impatient with a woman who stays in a violent situation, but as more than one woman said to me, "People don't know why you don't leave unless they've been in your shoes." Love is a strong force, and a woman can still love her husband even when she is in fear for her life. Most women wanting to resettle or redirect their lives face a long, uphill climb. The practical aspects of leaving often contribute to being ensnared. A job or a welfare check is needed, and it may take weeks of processing and waiting for money to be in hand. Housing, furnishings and transportation are necessary. And then of course, there is the problem of childcare. These are only the surface considerations. Low self-esteem, no work skills, and dependency further complicate things. Without supportive community the difficulty of leaving can be staggering.

A Particle of Light

Attentive and Ready

One of my prize keepsakes from this time is a small piece of cloth bearing a hand-sewn message stitched in green, purple and orange thread: "Fay Key loves God". It was made by a little girl who lived next door to Hospitality House. A volunteer had it framed for me, and I keep it on my desk, where I can be reminded regularly that once upon a time someone saw my deepest desire. I have wanted to love God, with heart and mind and soul and strength—with my whole self. I have fallen short, miserably at times, intentionally as well as unintentionally. The great, good news is not that I love God. It is that God loves me, loves each of us, loves all creation. God's love remains steadfast, even when our love fails.

Every day I prayed Morning Prayer and Night Prayer from the *Liturgy of the Hours*, followed by a period of silence. Almost always I did this alone, in the early morning and late at night. In the mornings I tried to spend time with one of the lectionary readings as well. The schedule of prayer, similar to the one Hannah and I kept at the House of Prayer, strengthened me for many a lonely or frightening time. And for all my years in the shelter I prayed Teresa of Avila's prayer after I got into bed at night:

> Let nothing disturb thee,
> Nothing affright thee;
> All things are passing;
> God never changeth;
> Patient endurance
> Attaineth to all things;
> Who God possesseth
> In nothing is wanting;
> Alone God sufficeth.[2]

Lessons from the Best of Teachers

My teachers taught me well. Tears, laughter, delight, disappointment, generosity, hard times, upset, sweetness, courage, all a part of life, they said. And life is good.

A precious four-year-old boy who lived near us visited me often. Answering the doorbell one summer day, I found him standing on the porch licking a juicy slice of red watermelon with unabashed enjoyment. When I invited him in he held it out to me saying, "My grandma sent this to you." I could well imagine her telling him not to take a bite of it. And he obeyed to the letter her request, but could not resist slurping some of that good juice. I took the slice of watermelon, cut it in half, and he and I ate it—our ritual celebration of the goodness of life.

Life is hard too, and asks hard questions that call for hard decisions. Love is nitty-gritty business. Jesus, drawing on his own spiritual heritage, says that two important commandments guide our lives: Love God. Love your neighbor. And in his living, Jesus tells us that to love God is to love your neighbor. Johannes Metz says, "Love of neighbor is not something different from love of God; it is merely the earthly side of the same coin. At their source they are one: that is the startling and distinctive note in the Christian message."[3] We all are trying to work out just what that means—and how to do it.

One hot July day two little boys arguing loudly came to see me. Both were trying to ask me a question. Finally, one out-shouted the other, "Fay, ain't you supposed to love your mama first and God second?" The other yelled, "No. You supposed to love God first and your mama second!" I was surprised at the question. Here were two runny-nosed, barefooted children arguing a serious theological question—and it was pretty important to them judging from the volume with which it was raised. I summoned my skills in diplomacy and told them they both were right in a way. I said, "We are supposed to love God with all that is in us, but the only way we have of showing that we love God is by loving people. If you love God, you will show it by loving your mama, and other people too—even people you don't particularly want to love." This was enough of a sermon. The two little boys turned to each other and said, "See, I told you!" And down the steps they went, continuing the argument. The learning is on-going. Love God; love your neighbor—the basis of our faith. Not two commandments. Only one. That is our hard reality.

At lunch one day a two-year-old sitting beside me bowed his head and said, "Jesus wept." I was stunned by his words as he placed truth on the table before us gathered for that meal. Jesus weeps when anyone is hurting or hungry in body, mind or spirit. Each day Jesus asks us to chant with him the Canticle of the Broken Heart for all whose lives are tangled in disorder and instability, who hunger for a better life.

Opened

The learning of those years was deeply personal, taking me to places in myself I did not want to go. From those years I know a little more clearly what it means to say "The light shines in the darkness, and the darkness did not overcome it."[4] It illuminates *everything* that needs to be seen and known, everything it is time for one to see and know, the broken and the beautiful.

From time to time life highlights our frailties and exposes our pretenses. God shines light into some dark corner of ourselves, determined to disillusion us and give us a good look at the reality of who we are. An illusion is always cracked from the outside: some concrete happening does the job. Ancient wisdom tells us that God's judgment is God's mercy. In the judgment new possibility is given.

A woman from our neighborhood and I were visiting in front of Hospitality House. As we talked, a drunk man came staggering toward us. He doubled over in pain and cried out for help. He clearly needed to get to the hospital, so I called a taxi to pick him up. When the taxi arrived the driver helped the sick man into the car, then turned to us and asked, "How is he going to pay me when we get there?" I stood quietly by with $12 in cash and a checkbook in my purse, consciously, deliberately refusing to answer that question. The woman beside me, meanwhile, put her last five dollar bill in the sick man's shirt pocket and said to the cab driver, "There's money in his shirt pocket. He can pay you when you get to the hospital." When I saw what she had done I immediately felt terrible disappointment in myself. I turned and hugged her as the cab pulled away. "We're all in the same boat," she said. I told a friend about what had happened, and she pointed out that this really was the story of the Good Samaritan acted out with me as the Levite. I had good friends like that. Anyone can see how ready I was to pass on by. I could see it, and it was painful.

This woman was Christ for me. This one by my side did not hesitate to give what was needed. She was the Word enfleshed. By her act I was judged. I saw my selfishness. I saw my willingness to let another bear the burden. I saw my attachment to my money and how attachment can stand between God and me. A peek at reality, and I wanted to close my eyes! But the judgment was mercy. In my seeing I was given a chance to change, to grow, to deepen in love—another chance to actively choose to live differently. She was the Word of Life saying,

A Particle of Light

"Take up your life and love it. Take up your situation and make the most of it." Incarnation is an affirmation of the human situation, not an escape from it. The downs, the ups, the glories, the tragedies, the joys, the sorrows—all are ours to use. We can say no to them or we can say yes to them. It is often a lonely decision.

Learning to Care

Our worth. It comes from God who is both Giver and Lover of life. Worth cannot be earned. Worth cannot be bought. It has nothing to do with the color of our skin; nothing to do with our family or our class; nothing to do with gender; nothing to do with our religion. Worth is not related to likes or dislikes, our practices or beliefs. Worth is a gift, God's gift to us. We belong to God, and therein lies our worth.

I was sitting in the yard with a mother and her two daughters, an African-American family. The older girl started calling me sister. The younger one asked if I were kin to them. I said, "Of course, we are all God's children." The older child then said "I wish everybody felt that way." I wished that too, from the depths of my being. Dignity and worth are God-given.

Late one September afternoon as I was preparing supper a young woman from our neighborhood called to ask if I could pick her up at the bus station. She was just returning from a long stay at Egleston Hospital in Atlanta, where her baby had been fighting for its life. "I've got my baby with me, and I can't manage both my bag and the baby," she said. I told her I would be right there. When I drove up to the station, she handed me the baby—a tiny thing, two months old and weighing only seven pounds. The baby's nose had been removed because of severe infection, and she was wheezing and gasping. I welcomed her home with hugs and kisses, then returned her to her mother's arms. As I looked at the mother and child, it struck me that in the eyes of the world this little blanketful of life most likely would be considered insignificant. To this thought, there came a grace-filled reply: As we were stopped at a traffic light on Broad Street, a big orange butterfly came to rest on the windshield immediately in front of the mother and her baby. It was a reminder for me that the favor of God rests in a special way on the poor and weak and defenseless ones of the earth. In the eyes of the world this little one might appear insignificant, but in the eyes of God, she is of supreme worth.

Learning was daily, daily, daily. One night I wrote in my journal: "Today's Gospel lesson was from Mark 10. The words 'not to be served, but to serve' have been with me all day. They are hard words to live by. I was aware during the day of times when I wanted to be served, to be loved, cared for, petted in some special way. Little jealousies, little hurts, irritability in myself seemed magnified in the light of these words. I prayed that I might become more like the One I follow in my limping way, the One who came not to be served, but to serve."

This simple thought came to me one day: serving means giving God glory by doing menial jobs in a spirit of joy. It resonated deeply and helped me see my tasks in a different light. What we so often term "menial" are the very things we can do to make life better for others. A child, after observing my daily activities—cleaning, making beds, cooking and serving meals, doing dishes—had found a category for me. As we were eating supper, I jumped up and down many times to get things people wanted—more ice, salt and pepper, another spoon, a glass of tea—and this little boy finally looked at me and said "You ain't nothin' but a maid. You just a servant." He was right, and I could embrace that. I was there to serve. The little tasks are important, and I wanted to do them well, to do them with love.

I also learned that to serve meant to comfort those who suffer—to comfort in the sense of offering consolation and solace, encouragement and strength. On the bulletin board in the kitchen I had pinned a picture of a statue I had seen at the Yad Vashem, Jerusalem's memorial to the Jewish war dead of World War II. When I first saw the statue its impact was so profound I fell to my knees. I felt as if I had been pressed down. It was Rachel, inconsolable over the massive slaughter of Holocaust. She was standing as witness to the powerless who were ravaged by the savagery of the powerful. Rachel in full lament, wailing and mourning for her children through the centuries—she who would not let herself be comforted stood before me. I knelt in silence before her.

Rachel weeps too, each day, for her suffering children hidden in the small, dark corners of the world. The women and children who stayed with us often bore heavy loads of concern, sorrow and fear. Their lives were desperately uncertain, the way forward hard. Often as I talked with a woman the thought would cross my mind, *her life is hard*. Many times I saw Rachel in anguish, weeping for her children, weeping over the sorrows of life. I heard God's words: "Comfort, O comfort my people. Comfort them."

Disciplined and Hopeful

At times I felt overwhelmed by the needs of people. We could do so little in the face of so much need. Our world was full of anguish, and our effort seemed slight. A question would creep into my consciousness from some dark place in me: Why do I bother doing this one little thing? Is it worth the effort? One afternoon when I was feeling discouraged I went out to sit in the backyard. The roar of traffic on South Broad was like an assault. As I sat there looking up through the glorious green of new spring leaves, I *saw* the blue sky alive with birds. Suddenly, even above the deafening siren of a passing ambulance, I *heard* the song of one single bird. I could hear it through all the noise. One single bird overcoming the many sounds of the busy street. I saw, I heard, I knew again the necessity of being faithful in little things. One bird singing. One song of joy. One person. One small act. That is enough.

Through the years at Hospitality House I thought a great deal about *hope*. Day after day I saw women resist despair. I saw women of hope rising each morning to face the challenges of the day. After being at the shelter for a few days a woman said to me, "I have come a long way from a suitcase and fear." That is a statement of hope. There is nothing of shallow optimism in it, no denial of darkness. Her tears were real. She had faced the terror of brutal family violence, but with a little help and support she had been able to see an alternative to a life of abuse. She somehow was able to see through and beyond to the promise of light on the distant horizon. Perhaps seeing light in the distance allows us to look honestly at the darkness of the present situation and even see the possibility and potential in it. Hope engenders courage. It keeps us going; it keeps us in the struggle; it keeps us faithful to the task of working on present problems.

In the early morning every day, as light comes and scatters the darkness, the Christian Church prays with Zechariah:

> In the tender compassion of our God
> the dawn from on high shall break upon us,
> to shine on those who dwell in darkness

and the shadow of death,
and to guide our feet into the way of peace.[5]

This I believe. Credo. I would put my money on this. Maybe even my life.

Through all the years at the shelter I held in my heart the idea of starting a House of Prayer. I knew that was what I was to do. I also knew that this period was my long sojourn in the land of preparation, and I was to give myself to it. I loved life at Hospitality House. It was good for me, and I learned more than I can ever say. But I could feel the push onward growing stronger.

Entering the Birth Canal

One evening in the quiet dark just before going to bed three images came slowly and clearly to me—images of encounter with God.

In the first, the Lion of Judah has me by the scruff of the neck in his strong sharp teeth. He shakes me this way and that until I am forced to let go of all I clutch and cling to, leaving me empty and defenseless.

In the second, the Great Feathered Wings cover me and all is dark beneath their brightness. I sing for joy in the shadow of God's wings.

In the third image, I bow low, my face to the ground, with a full, dark cape covering me. I am in the presence of the Sun of Righteousness and dare not look upon it. I am not righteous. In grace He burns me with His brightness. His holiness heals me. He lifts me up. He alone can make me holy, bright, righteous. I am overcome with love for this One who loves me without condition.

These images seemed a profound personal truth being given to me in the darkness of the moment. I felt that no action was being asked of me. I was to hold them, to sit quietly with them, trusting that in time light would be shed on them.

I was in a period of struggle. My clay was being molded by what often seemed a rough hand. Yet I was certain that Love was behind it all. God was pursuing me, that old Lion with the sharp teeth—drawing me into commitment deeper than I could grasp. I was being asked to let go of anything that stood in the way. Indeed, I was being grasped by what I could not grasp.

As a young woman I had been "head over heels" in love a few times. Even at this time in my mid-30's there was a man tugging at my heart. I often went to the library and wandered among the stacks when I needed to sort something out. One day, as I stood alone in the quiet space between hundreds of books, my attention was drawn by the one nearest my hand, *A Track to the Water's Edge: The Olive Schreiner Reader*. I had just read about this book in Howard Thurman's autobiography, *With Head and Heart*. I pulled the book off the shelf and opened it. My eyes fell on words that I knew were meant for me: "Take the shoes of dependence off your feet." I closed the book and stood quietly for a long while. By the time I had walked back to Hospitality House I had come to clarity around a calling to celibacy, and it was hard. I felt sad that I would never again feel the joy of a lover's kiss. Those words seemed so final, and the remembered pleasure seemed even more seductive. I felt even sadder that this decision would mean laying aside the possibility of having my own family. Even so, I knew I would not change course. I wrote in my journal: "The pleasures of my God are more alluring to me—harsh, wild, high and glorious. And praise wells up within, fierce, unbidden. I have been called, my name sounded out. "You are mine," God has said. This is sweet beyond the telling. To see as His, thus mine, all the world of nature burning with beauty. Sights and sounds caressing my senses. The reaching hands of children. The embracing arms of mothers. The good voices of friends. All mine, for I am His." I was being shaken, forced to let go of all I was trying to cling to. And I was singing for joy under God's wings.

The third image is straight from the book of Malachi.[6] One morning the lectionary presented me with it. God comes like a refiner's fire, and who can endure it? Yet, if we endure, Malachi assures us, God refines our faith and turns our gifts into silver and gold. And the sun of righteousness will rise with healing in its wings.

Who can bear that Presence? Yet I had to bear it. I was being made ready. I awoke daily to the needs of the shelter. The kitchen floor had to be mopped, the precious children must be cared for, the suffering mothers needed comforting, the meals had to be made—the endless needs of the daily round, all had to be dealt with again and again. It was wearing—burning me like refiner's fire. I wrote in my journal that day: "Teach me to pray. Enable me to love. Keep me faithful. So much stands between us. Remove it. I want You, God. Fill me."

And in the midst of the struggle some sweetness always came. One rainy night after sitting down for supper the doorbell rang. A volunteer answered it, and I could hear a child asking, "Is Fay here?" The volunteer said, "She's eating supper." The child replied, "I have to see her." In came a young neighborhood boy wearing a blue slicker. He walked up to my chair and said, "Fay, I love you." I was touched to the core by the love and openness of this child. "I have to see her"—as if he had been sent by God with that particular message for me. And I believe he had.

Lessons from the Best of Teachers

Further Clarification of Direction

Someone brought me a book entitled *Wide Neighborhoods* by Mary Breckinridge who founded the Frontier Nursing Service in Appalachia in the early 20th century. In the book the author told of visiting an "anchoress" in England. Breckinridge, crushed by the tragic death of her small son, had been unable to move forward with the work of founding the Nursing Service. When she visited the anchoress, they talked for two hours about the love and goodness of God. She told of the healing power of her visit with this woman of prayer, the peace, the calm, the refreshment of energy which she experienced as they sat together. After this meeting she began to emerge from her dark night of grief, integrating her loss into her larger life. No longer crippled by her sorrow, she found courage to again pick up the work she was called to do. My tears flowed as I read the account. I recognized in it my own calling to deep prayer and was set on the way to the next part of my journey. I began calling the apartment we had rented for staff space and retreat the Anchorhold. When I told Betty, my divinity school roommate, she sent me an anchor doorknocker, a gift which would be used in a future setting.

Things seemed to be moving fast, in a way that was pushing me forward into what lay ahead. One day as I was praying in the apartment, I received four words that seemed to inform my direction: Vision. Prayer. Community. Service. Though I felt I was already living out of those words, it seemed clear that I needed to pay attention. I wrote them down and allowed them to take up residence in me. I told Betty about this, and she said, "Perhaps you are being called to start a religious community." Something in that resonated, but the possibility seemed far-fetched.

A Particle of Light

I made a retreat under the direction of Fr. John Hugo in Pittsburgh. The retreat was a preached version of the Spiritual Exercises of St. Ignatius, combining several conferences each day with time for praying Scripture. In brief, the retreat was designed to invite and challenge people to live a holy life in the midst of the world. This meant not only trying to avoid sin, but also choosing the "more," the better above the good— and choosing always for love of God. Fr. Hugo was a close friend of Sr. Hannah's. At Hannah's suggestion Dorothy Day attended the retreat in 1941, after which Fr. Hugo became her spiritual director. Hannah kept insisting that I make the retreat, so I did. It was my first week-long silent retreat.

One day Fr. Hugo presented the Joseph story from Genesis as prayer material. I sat quietly, alone in my room, reading how Joseph had disclosed himself to his brothers, weeping over them and embracing them—accepting the very brothers who had sold him into slavery.[7] As I sat there some words came clearly into my mind: *AN ETHER OF ACCEPTING PRESENCE*. A few moments later those resonant words came again: *AN ETHER OF ACCEPTING PRESENCE*. As I sat still, the words settling around and in me, I had a strong sense of being accepted by God, by God's whole creation—as if I were being held in an atmosphere suffused with love. And it was not just *I* being held in that love, it was *everything*, the whole universe. Then came a dawning sense of what I was to be. I was to be an ether of accepting presence for others. I was being asked to become a conscious part of that mysterious atmosphere of love suffusing all that is. *Love with My Love*. My heart said, "Yes." That was all the instruction I got that day.

A few months later, near the end of December, my mother died after a long, hard bout with cancer. Steve Bullington came to her funeral and said again that he was interested in working with me. Our lives were now intertwined, and I knew we were to be soulmates. I suggested that he move to Rome and become a part of the Hospitality House community. That was not to be. I returned to Rome on January 1, 1986, and almost immediately knew it was time for me to leave. On the spiritual journey, one sometimes experiences a collusion of inner and outer forces, pushing and pulling one along. Upon my return to Hospitality House there was not only an interior push onward, there was an outer one as well.

For a couple of years several of the Board members had been pressing us toward a social work model for the shelter. I have high regard for social workers, but I knew I was not called to be one. Hospitality House had been founded as a small Christian community that was to be a presence of love and support for the women and their children who needed us. I was against this change of direction for the shelter. This was a painful time. Misunderstandings grew around this division, and I could feel the ground shifting. I loved my life at the shelter. I loved living in Rome. But it grew increasingly clear that the time was drawing near for me to leave the shelter and turn to the new work I was clearly being called to do. My imagination, of course, turned toward a House of Prayer—the dream I had been holding in my heart for years. My good friend Fran was moving away from Rome, and on the day she left she stopped to say good-bye. As we stood on the walkway in front of Hospitality House I told her that I had a strong sense that it was time for me to begin a House of Prayer and that I wanted to do that in rural south Georgia. As I described my very rudimentary vision of the place she listened carefully and said, "I can just see you doing that." It was the blessing I needed.

I was in grief over my mother's death and knew I should not make any decision about moving until my grief abated and I was more at peace. Leaving Hospitality House felt like leaving my child. But the sense of urgency to move toward a prayer ministry grew ever stronger. I had saved $1,000, so I put it in a savings account as seed money, under the name "Green Leaf." And one day at the monastery in Conyers I bought a sandcasting of a dove with a leaf in its beak. I wrapped it in tissue paper and put it in the back of my closet—my promise that I would be ready when the time was right.

Time to Go

One Sunday morning in February, 1986 the shelter was full of women and children. The television was blaring. A wrestling match was on. I took my journal, sat on my bed and began to pray and write. I said to God, "This is how I feel inside—*I'm wrestling*. I believe it is time for me to go, but I can't make the decision at this point. So if You want me to make a move toward starting a House of Prayer, then You had better make it very clear." I went on to say, "And this is how You can make it clear." I asked that gifts to Hospitality House in memory of my mother reach a certain figure, and I quoted a figure higher than I thought possible. Then I said that I wanted to be asked to lead a retreat by Mothers' Day, knowing that anyone having a retreat in early May would have all the plans made by this time. I left it at that.

I had been invited to attend a United Methodist Women's Quadrennial Meeting in Anaheim, California, in late March. While I was there I prayed and prayed. The feeling of being squeezed into a new life was strong. The day after I returned from Anaheim to Rome a check came in the mail putting me two dollars over what I had asked for. The day after that I had a call from a United Methodist woman in south Georgia. She said "We have had Bishop Marjorie Matthews (the first woman bishop in the United Methodist Church) lined up for two years to be our retreat speaker, and she has been hospitalized with cancer and can't come. Is there any way that you could come at such late notice?" I said, "Oh, yes. I'll be there." Steve came for a visit sometime in the middle of this period, and I told him the time had come for me to start a House of Prayer. He said he wanted to be a part of it. That felt like an exclamation of affirmation to me. God's, "GO!" The time had come to make a move.

I have felt that my mother was midwife to this new birth. Before she died she asked me, "Do you think you might ever come back to south Georgia?" I answered, "Mama, that is up to God." She then said that Steve's mother, Margaret Bullington, had visited her and told her that Steve wanted to work with me, and she thought that was a good idea. I liked the idea too, but said that decision was out of my hands. When I heard that Bishop Matthews had to cancel because of cancer, I felt the situation held some clear message from my mother. Then, of course, there was the land itself that provided a place to start a House of Prayer, a gift that came directly after her death. Her encouraging presence seemed real to me.

Once the decision had been made to begin a House of Prayer, I turned in my resignation to Hospitality House. I did it with a mix of emotions. I felt the sorrow of leaving a place and a people so dear to my heart and also the welling excitement and joy of responding to God's initiative, the exhilaration of moving into the unknown. Some words attributed to St. Francis of Assisi sustained me many times while living at the shelter, and they saw me through as I left Rome:

> Do not worry if the fight seems unduly great and the work unsupportable, for the reward is great in proportion to them. Do not lose your confidence for an instant. Run with love into

the midst of the fight. God is all-powerful. The things you have undertaken to do are far beyond your strength to accomplish, but God has promised to see you through, and God's word is truth.[8]

Steve, who was serving as pastor of a United Methodist Church in South Georgia, told me he would finish his appointment year in June and could move at that point. In the meantime, there were things I needed to do in preparation.

I sent the news of my plans to family and friends. Hannah (Sr. Peter Claver) immediately wrote back saying I should pursue the training in spiritual direction at the Jesuit Center for Spiritual Growth in Wernersville, Pennsylvania. My friend, Sr. Rita, had already suggested that I make a 30-day retreat based on the Spiritual Exercises of St. Ignatius, and I knew that was my next step. It seemed the best possible way of letting go of Hospitality House and turning toward whatever God was calling me to do with a House of Prayer.

As it turned out, the thirty-day retreat prerequisite for entering the training program in spiritual direction, presented a problem. It was already July and the training in Pennsylvania ran January-June—yet the Center in Wernersville did not offer a 30-day retreat again until the next summer. I did not know where to turn. In the middle of this dilemma my friend Betty stopped for a visit on her way to see her mother in Birmingham. She promised she would be praying with me. Two days later a brochure arrived in the mail. She had seen it in a Catholic Church and thought I might be interested. It was a retreat schedule from the Jesuit Spirituality Center in Grand Coteau, Louisiana, offering 30-day retreats almost monthly. I applied that day for one beginning in September—perfect timing. And so it was that I left Rome.

Chapter 9

Days of Prayer, Months of Training

Praying through the Spiritual Exercises of St. Ignatius was a powerful experience. By the end of those thirty days I felt my heart was ready for whatever God wanted of me. Near the end of the retreat I opened a small book of daily readings, and the one for that particular day was from Rainer Maria Rilke: "You must give birth to your images. They are your future waiting to be born…fear not the strangeness you feel. The future must enter into you long before it happens.…" I thought of the long-ago image of a house that seemed so important to me. I had carried that image without knowing what it was about, and suddenly I understood. All the houses that were a part of my life in Rome—the House of Prayer, Hospitality House, Hope House, Mary and Martha's—were in some sense 'the house,' but this house about to come into being was *the* house. The others were precursors, equipping me for what lay ahead.

As soon as I left the retreat I applied for the Wernersville program for training in spiritual direction, a January to June residential program.

They told me I was applying very late and that they already had accepted three interns and were not too interested in having a fourth. On *that* encouraging note I was asked to come for personal interviews with the staff on November 1st and 2nd, All Saints' Day and All Souls' Day, 1986. I remember two days of luminous golden leaves on trees and grounds, against a background of gray drizzle. I enjoyed meeting the staff and talking with each of them. Between interviews I sat in the chapel under the stained-glass window depicting St. Martha. I had never seen a window honoring St. Martha—but there she was holding a ladle and a big ring of keys, the householder. I felt fiercely my mother Martha's presence with me. It was less than a year after her death. She had wanted me to return to south Georgia to start a House of Prayer, and I felt sure she was praying for me as I sought a way to bring that dream into reality. I was accepted.

The training was more than I could have hoped for. Being a resident at the Jesuit Center, living in community with the staff and three other interns, directing retreatants under supervision of wonderful mentors—it was preparation of the highest quality. And the gift of money I had been given as I left Hospitality House just covered the cost of the program plus an airline ticket.

One other unexpected gift of my time in Wernersville came near the end of the program. Fr. Bob Hamm, head of the Center, told me that he had a dear friend in Georgia. When I asked who it was he said it was Joe Way, an Episcopal priest. Incredibly, Joe had taught at Swainsboro High School when I was a student there. Though I never had him as a teacher I remembered him well. He later became an Episcopal priest. Joe had been to Wernersville on retreat, and Bob Hamm was his director. They stayed in touch and visited back and forth for years. Bob had actually been to Swainsboro with Joe. He suggested that Joe might be helpful to me in starting a House of Prayer. As soon as I returned to Georgia I called Joe, and Steve and I went to talk with him. I asked Joe to be my spiritual director. I felt placed in his hands, and his friendship was a truly great gift to both Steve and me. His support, encouragement and wisdom steadied and guided us. He understood what a House of Prayer meant.

Chapter 10

A New Life - Green Bough

There is something humorous about taking the leap of faith and landing in Scott, Georgia. An early visitor commented, "You surely must have been called by God. Why else would you have come to this place to live?" Truly it was in response to God's call that Steve and I came here. The place is very ordinary—no majestic mountains, no roaring sea, no grand lake or expansive rolling hills. It lies on the edge of wiregrass country where a lot of the landscape is flat and scrubby. I sometimes say there is nothing here but God. The magnificence of this land is subtle, but give it a while and it will steal your heart. It was only after I had lived here for a cycle of seasons that my eyes were opened to see the astonishing beauty of this spot—the water oaks, pines and pecan trees; the broom sedge; the hydrangeas and the wild daffodils that bloom year after year, planted by generations past; the bluebirds, cardinals, mockingbirds and bob-whites, the whippoorwills and tiny brown wrens; the wind that blows with both strength and caressing gentleness, clouds that scud overhead and night skies that are breathtaking. It is here in this middle-Georgia landscape that God has whispered to me, "You shall be called My Delight Is in Her, and your land Married."[1]

A New Life - Green Bough

When my mother died I inherited this property. With my brother Denny's approval I decided to offer a portion of the land to God, returning the gift that had been given to me. Steve and I came to this place and this work with a burning longing to love with abandon the God who first loved us. We came with the understanding that our calling was two-fold. First of all, we were here to pray and to be a presence of prayer, whether anyone else ever came or not. Second, we were here to provide sacred space for others to come and pray, if that was what God wanted.

Who would ever come to Scott? That was a hard question. But I knew that I was to start this House of Prayer, and as I understood it, those who came would be entirely up to God. In fact, I still say to people who come here, "You would never have come to Scott unless God brought you. There is no other reason for you to come." Long before arriving here I began praying, "God, bring people who need to come, and bring people we need to have come." Steve and I continue to pray this prayer. Thirty years have passed. People have come! Wonderful people. It just happened.

Steve and I began work on the property on June 24, 1987, Feast of John the Baptist. We were young (I was 45 and Steve 33), clear-eyed, vigorous, open—and wholly in love with God. We found shoulder-high weeds, a shabby old house and a caved-in chicken coop. I said, "We may be eating locusts and wild honey before this is over." With sling-blades we worked our way from the road to the house. Then over the next few weeks, with the help of family and friends, we made the house habitable. I stayed in Swainsboro, and Steve lived in an old trailer near Interstate-16. We met at Green Bough early each morning, began our day together with Morning Prayer, and then set to work, reclaiming inch by inch, this lovely piece of land. Our purpose, of course, was to create a place of prayer.

It had been almost ten years since I had made my first visit to a House of Prayer. Providence guided me there. Sr. Peter Claver invited me in. As we sat together and talked and prayed, I felt an enormous sense of relief and reassurance. God's goodness and love enfolded me. All that had gone on in my life had prepared me for the day when I knew that God wanted me to love Him, not for gain, but out of sheer devotion—heart, soul, mind, strength. "Seek, and you will find," Jesus told us. Most passers-by did not even notice that house, but for me the Star stopped over it. For me it was holy ground. The daily round of prayer that went on there made it sacred and opened a channel for God's grace, making it easy for others to come and pray. Our world needs places like Green Bough, for prayer is the very breath of the life of faith.

So it was that Steve and I came to pray and to set apart this land as a quiet place where others could come aside to be still and listen. We had a vision for this place, but I am very sure that neither of us could have imagined that it would flourish in the way that it has. We called the place Green Bough.

What's in a Name?

In embryonic phase, while I was still living in Rome, I called it Green Leaf. Long before my lifetime there was a small Methodist Church near Swainsboro called Green Leaf. My friend Kay was looking through a book on the history of Methodism in Emanuel County and came upon a sentence about this old church. She pointed out the reference and said, "That's a lovely name, isn't it." I agreed and began thinking that Green Leaf might be a good name for a House of Prayer. It reminded me of the Noah story when the dove returns to the ark with a green leaf symbolizing God's ever-faithful action of reconciling outreach to earth and its inhabitants. And it called up for me the glorious vision of the New Jerusalem in the book of Revelation where the leaves of the tree of life are for the healing of the nations. As it turned out an organization was already incorporated under the name Green Leaf so another had to be chosen. In 1987 before leaving Pennsylvania, I visited my friend Betty in Pittsburgh. We spent a day at a small House of Prayer outside the city. Beside the chapel door hung a holy water font with a Chinese proverb engraved on it: "If I keep a green bough in my heart the singing bird will come." I recognized the new name immediately. Green Leaf became Green Bough.

The meaning of the name has continued to grow. In 1993 Sr. Peter Claver came from Philadelphia for a visit. As we were driving her back to the Atlanta airport she began telling me about the work of Fr. John LaFarge and mentioned his autobiography, *The Manner is Ordinary*. After we had seen her off, Steve and I stopped by a used bookstore in Atlanta. I had barely stepped inside when I saw that very book staring at me from a shelf. I brought it home and put it by my chair where it stayed unopened for several weeks. When I did 'take and read' (on September 15, 1993 according to a margin note on page 108) I came upon LaFarge's story of visiting the Assisi hillside with a friend. As they walked they came upon an old shepherd who was unsuccessfully trying to drive a sheep along by whacking it on the rear with a stick. As he watched the shepherd he recalled a lecture on St. Augustine's treatise on "Grace" that he had heard several months earlier. Augustine says that we are drawn by love, moved to Christ by delight: delight in the truth, in blessedness, justice, eternal life. "Show me a lover, and he knows what I am talking about," said Augustine. "Show a green bough to a sheep and you draw it after you." The beauty, truth and goodness of Christ delight us, attract us, compel us to follow. LaFarge broke off a leafy apple bough, gave it to the shepherd and told him to wave it before the sheep. The sheep began to follow the shepherd, and off they went.[2] This seemed a wonderful unfolding of the name of our place. Christ is the green bough who draws us to God. By extension we all are meant to be green boughs—God's great delights, who in our living show forth the love, beauty, goodness and truth of Christ in a way that draws others to God. Along my journey I have been blessed by many green boughs who have drawn me ever deeper into the heart of God. For them I am profoundly grateful.

A friend, having heard me tell this story, gave us a copy of *Prince of Egypt*, an animated film about Moses and the Exodus. She said, "Watch for the little boy with the green bough." And sure enough, in the long line of slaves crossing into freedom, there he was riding on the back of a cart, smiling and holding a green bough. A sheep was following.

A name is important. It reveals and calls forth something of the essence of what is named. In calling this place Green Bough we are saying that we are here to pray because we believe prayer is vital to faith. And we are here to extend an invitation to others, "Come and see. Let Love draw you in too. We all belong to God."

Houses

I do not know what it is about houses, but they have figured large in my life. I have loved all the houses I have lived in from childhood on, containers of daily life. I have loved all the houses that have come forth from my work. Now there is Green Bough.

A New Life - Green Bough

Looking back I can see that childhood play was anticipating the direction of my future. I wonder now what was already in motion as I played with my blocks, lost in the joy of building houses with those scraps of left-over lumber from my grandfather's workshop. Had I been able to look forward, I might have seen that this creative play, imagining, building, was preparing me for my future work. It makes perfect sense to me that it was. I am convinced that we come into this life on earth with God-given purpose. Our particular time and place are not randomly given us. We come into life with unique gifts and callings planted in us like seeds. The seeds lie in darkness, deep within us, waiting, breaking open in due time; to grow, to flower and to bear fruit as we mature. I can feel this in my own life.

I have enjoyed my relationship with houses. They are the stuff—at least the material stuff—of my life. Houses to be reclaimed, or built, or appointed in a welcoming way. I think it is safe for me to say that the houses of my life culminate in Green Bough. It is *the* house in my life. It has held me in a way no other has. It is the house that points directly to HOME, which is another name for God. Most days I still feel that joy of creative play in a world that, I must admit, is far more mysterious than I can imagine. What lies ahead? I don't know, so I will take time to remember and reflect.

Chapter 11

The Houses and the History of Green Bough

The Old House: 1987

In 1987 the only standing structure on the property was a small 1920s farmhouse sitting in a field of neck-high weeds. My grandfather had built it long ago for use as a tenant farmhouse. Though it was not much to look at, we found it sturdy and the foundation sure. The rusty tin roof and peeling tarpaper siding spoke of another era. I was enchanted by its simplicity. Of low estate, and with scars fully exposed, it seemed to say, "Come sit a spell with me, and let me teach you something about patient endurance. You live in a fast-paced age that values what is instant and disposable. Let me tell you about the timeless values of steadfastness and overcoming." When I showed my dear friend Hannah a picture of this house her comment was, "What a wonderfully humble beginning."

I loved this humble house from the start. It was a "fixer-upper." The general disrepair of the place attested to that. But it had possibility! I could look at it with one eye squint and see it full of promise. As a human being I could identify with its condition. We all are "fixer-uppers" in need of another chance. I, myself, had been fixed up—refreshed after weariness, cleaned up after making a mess, encouraged when disheartened, forgiven of shortcomings, held by Love when I felt unlovable. This house was asking for another chance.

An old handyman, who could jimmy and patch and make-it-up-as-he-went, lived nearby. His price was phenomenally low. He helped us with many projects over the years. He and Steve would slide on their bellies under the house to lay or repair pipes and climb to the top of the roof to work on leaks or put screens over the chimneys. The two of them together worked patiently, loving and cajoling the old house into usefulness.

Barely a month after we began work the bills came in. I wrote in my journal on July 29: "The first bills came in today. I was afraid I was way over my limit, expecting a $1,500 one from Swainsboro Supply. I opened it and found it was $1,145.58. I rejoiced, because my money market account has $1,142.79 in it, and when interest is added for the month it will just cover this bill. Thank You, God." So often it was this way.

The interior of the house needed much work. It was dirty and flea-infested. Several family members and a couple of work teams came to help with stripping, scraping and scrubbing as we made an advance toward a habitable space. It was mid-July, and I wanted to move in by early September. Over the next few weeks, after painting the walls, my heart began to feel lighter. Friends in Swainsboro gave us kitchen flooring and a new kitchen stove. As soon as the flooring was laid, the kitchen was so inviting I knew I was home. I put some flowers on the mantel and began moving in some furniture. On September 7, we brought in a bed that had belonged to my Key grandparents, a chest of drawers and a few chairs. The next day, with the help of Steve's sister and brother-in-law, Sue and Bill Bagwell (Bill is also my cousin), we were able to get my Carter grandparents' old oak dining table cleaned up and moved in. Steve cooked a meal for us. Following dinner we were joined by my father and step-mother Helen, my brother Denny and sister-in-law Peggy. The eight of us celebrated our first Eucharist in the house. It was September 8, 1987, Feast of the Birth of Mary—10 years to the day since I had moved into the House of Prayer in Rome. Steve and I were full of gratitude and excitement.

The promise of Green Bough had become reality. I could now hang the sandcast dove I had bought at the monastery several years before. I placed it by the front door of the Old House, where it hangs to this day.

We had little money and had to work at things slowly, project-to-project, as we could afford it. I was very careful about not getting into debt. One time we had a leak under the kitchen sink and had to use a small bucket to catch the water. As the leak grew larger, I found that I needed to empty the bucket several times a day. Finally, I said, "Steve, we need to get a larger bucket." Steve said, "No, we need to have the leak fixed." He was right. Always something was needing attention. Property requires upkeep!

One of our early Associates volunteered the expert carpentry skills of her husband. He came with her annually for over 20 years, renovating, building, updating—making all our property better than we ever could have imagined. With the acquisition of houses over time has come more and more responsibility for the upkeep of property. The task of caretaking is ongoing.

Today this house looks much the same as it did 30 years ago. Though we have painted the tin roof, nailed down the tarpaper siding and replaced the front porch, the structure of the house is unchanged. Clearly the same old unpretentious and inviting ambience abides. Nearly everyone says at some point, "This reminds me of my grandmother's place. My grandparents' house was where I felt safest and most loved. I knew I *belonged* there. I feel as if I have come home." This house we have refurbished bears a spirit of welcome. It came to be called the Old House and holds the place of Mother House in Green Bough's history. It has spoken of its values to hundreds of people.

I lived in the Old House for 17 years. We loved one another, and when the time came for me to move, I left it reluctantly.

The Hermitage of St. John the Baptist: 1988

In the summer of 1988 we were ready to build a house for Steve. Over the course of several weeks we walked around the property, looking for just the right place to build a hermitage. One day we literally stumbled on the foundation of an old tobacco barn covered by vines. As we pulled the overgrowth away we discovered that it was a sound foundation and about the right size for a small frame house. It was in a lovely wooded area not too far away from the Old House. Steve felt it was a good spot for him to live. We cleared the space and spent time envisioning a dwelling, which he named The Hermitage of St. John the Baptist. He reflected:

But why 'hermitage'? Because in 1988, as in John the Baptist's and Jesus' day, hearing tends to grow dull in the busy noisiness without and within us. Because in his words and in his living, Jesus made clear that life towards the Kingdom calls for focusing and continual refocusing. "The Spirit immediately drove him out into the wilderness.... And in the morning a great while before day, he rose and went out to a lonely place, and there he prayed." Kingdom life means singleness of eye and heart, and that requires the practice of 'a lonely place.'[1]

For a year Steve had been camping out in a very rough trailer near Interstate-16. Its only redeeming quality was that it was free. He drove the twelve miles on dirt roads every day, dodging chickens and cows, arriving at Green Bough in time for Morning Prayer before our workday began. After putting in a full day of work on the property we would share a light supper, pray Night Prayer together, and then I would see him off for his twelve-mile trip back to his trailer. Several months of this daily routine made it clear that it was time to build a house on the property for Steve. Plans and work ensued. With the help of some of his friends from Tifton and two volunteer work teams, we began building the Hermitage of St. John the Baptist—a one-room house with bathroom and screened porch.

We soon discovered something about the hermitage that, after all these years, still makes me laugh. In trying to maximize the space, we had minimized the closet. It was so small the coat hangers could not hang straight. This little house has been a good place for Steve to live, but in the experience of building this simple structure we learned a valuable lesson: for any building that might follow, we were going to need professional help!

We were able to get the house ready for him to move into on December 10, 1988, the 20th anniversary of Thomas Merton's death. We both had been influenced by the life and writing of this Trappist monk, and we felt it a fitting day for Steve to take up hermitage life. This was our way of honoring Merton who, in the 1960s, had lived in a hermitage at the Abbey of Gethsemani in Kentucky.

Steve moved into the hermitage on the Saturday before the third Sunday of Advent. In the late afternoon we prayed Evening Prayer there in the glow of three burning candles. We read the lessons appointed for the day, calling us to "Rejoice!" The Gospel lesson brought us the strong words of John the Baptist, "There is One coming after me.... I am not worthy to unfasten his sandals." Then we read a piece about Merton and then some of Merton's own writings—a beautiful way to end the special day. Steve spent his first night there that night, and I was happy to have him close by.

One day, in a playful mood, Steve added a swing nearby, hanging it from the limb of a tall, shady tree. It evokes memories of childhood, and hardly anyone who sees it can resist swinging for a while—shades of the grandparents' house.

My favorite hermit in all the world lives in the Hermitage of St. John the Baptist.

Our friend, Joe Way, asked me to speak at the church he served in Augusta. As a thank-you he gave me a small photograph of Merton in his hermitage at Gethsemani. A Catholic Sister who had visited Merton had snapped the picture just as he was consecrating the host. She had given the photograph to Joe, who gave it to me. After getting it framed, it occurred to me that it should hang in the hermitage here at Green Bough. It seemed a perfect way of tying the two places together.

Procession of Blessing: Celebrating the Beginning

On March 27, 1988, Palm Sunday, with the Old House in good shape, the Hermitage dried-in and St. Joseph's Shed set in place for storage, we were ready to dedicate the property for use. About seventy people, family and friends, showed up for the blessing. It was a close-to-perfect afternoon, with sunshine, wind, singing birds, and yellow daffodils. A friend of my mother's decked the Old House with peach blossoms, wild plum and palm branches.

Joe Way was celebrant for the event. We began at the front entrance of the Old House, moving through the space, blessing each room with prayer, incense and a liberal sprinkling of holy water. As we came out the back door we fell into a long line, slowly moving to the tool shed, on to the Hermitage of John the Baptist, and from there to the edge of the field to bless the land itself. We processed through that glorious afternoon, under the blue March sky. Billowing clouds sailed overhead like presences from another sphere. Heaven and earth seemed full of God's glory.

Processions move me deeply. The ritual of that slow, forward movement of people taps into the wonder of being a part of something that spans time and space, something so large and so long it is beyond comprehension. It ties me into the procession of creation from the beginning of the beginning, calling me to a profound sense of my place in the flow of life—particularly as a human being, one of the marchers in the long, winding line of those who have lived, are living and will live.

The Houses and the History of Green Bough

In procession I can see the expansiveness of *journey*. I can imagine a little more clearly what "was in the beginning, is now and ever shall be." The long march of life comes into focus, from its most basic form, right through the arduous struggle of human beings coming to consciousness, and pointing ahead to what the future will hold. An ancient gate opens in me, connecting me to the birth, the suffering, the death, the sorrows and joys, hopes and fears and dreams, the losses and fulfillments that bear us along. I experience procession as a ritual blessing of the gift of Life.

One night I had a powerful dream of Steve and me sitting in a long hallway. We sat on the floor with our backs to the wall watching people pass by. I watched as men straggled by individually and in small clusters. Then as I looked in the distance I could see many more people coming along. I suddenly knew it was time to rise and give honor. I said to Steve, "We must stand now, the women are passing by." I was moved to tears as they passed. Some of them I knew well, catching their eyes, nodding in recognition, speaking their names. Others were unknown to me. They were from different times and places, different races and religions, some rich, some poor, but I knew deep in my heart that all of these were the ones who had carried the daily burdens of life, the losses of children and spouses and dear friends. All of their past must be honored: their longing for peace to supplant war; their desire for healing to spring from brokenness; and their nurturing spirits and strong shoulders that carried so many. They were the steady, faithful faces of love. I saw them, and I bowed low and reverently as they passed by. Conscious or unconscious, we all are a part of the great procession. We are called to attend, with open eyes and reverence, to Life. We are called to struggle hard to finish the work of those gone before, to make a way for Life to move forward.

Green Bough and all who are a part of it are caught up in that procession. And every small procession in this place, in our liturgies and celebrations and daily meanderings, calls us to attention. OPEN YOUR EYES AND SEE WHAT YOU ARE A PART OF!

When we consecrated Green Bough, we consecrated life and land for this.

The Retreat House: 1991

We thought of Green Bough as a still, quiet place where people could sit in silence and solitude and learn again their own true identity; a restful place where one could ask the right questions (for true rest is wanting what God wants). We were ready to share this place and our life together here with others.

By 1989 it was clear that the second part of our calling was beginning to emerge. People had begun to come—family and friends at first, then by word of mouth news spread and others began to come. When several people wanted to make retreat we had to rent space at one of the nearby campgrounds—not ideal for silent, directed retreats. It was time for us to look into building a retreat house at Green Bough. On Monday, May 1, Feast of Joseph the Worker, I placed a hammer on the altar in the Old House, and we began praying for guidance in building a new house.

A number of people had encouraged us to incorporate and apply for tax exempt status with the IRS. I was reluctant to make this move, but counsel from some wise friends pressed me along. We began the long process.

Our first step was to set up a small board of directors to support the work here. Fran Shaw and Joe Way agreed to serve as board members for this fledgling house. Fran, a deeply trusted friend of many years, had served as Chair of the Hospitality House Board when I was in Rome. I knew I wanted and needed her to be a part of this new venture. I knew, too, that Joe, who had become both dear friend and spiritual director for the two of us here, would be of immense help in guiding the formation of Green Bough. So, along with Steve and me, our first little board-of-four was organized. Some years later, after Joe's death, Mary Alice Kemp became the fourth member of the board, and soon after that we added a fifth member, Rob Townes. When Mary Alice had to resign, Beth Knowlton followed her.

After establishing the board we contacted the IRS. We were guided through an involved process lasting many months. A helicopter used to move slowly over the Old House in the early evening, and we would say it was the IRS checking us out. The process turned out to be very helpful, forcing us to set down on paper a clearer delineation of our vision. We have made use of that work through the years. An old friend who was visiting me mentioned that his wife was a lawyer who specialized in incorporating non-profits. He suggested that I talk to her. When I asked her for help she responded immediately and graciously. On December 20, 1989, we received our Book of Incorporation, and in early 1990 we received a letter from the IRS with our official tax-exempt number.

It was time to build. Our imaginations turned toward the kind of space we needed. I began drawing a building plan of sorts. A rectangle that grew longer with each new idea, it contained guest rooms, baths, chapel, library/sitting room, with a kitchen bar. Steve said, "It's going to look like a chicken house." So I called an architect friend who sat down with us, looked at what we showed him, pointed out that there were three functions, made a few magic moves and within a minute had laid out the plan for what is now the Green Bough Retreat House.

The way was unfolding—a builder appeared, a few extra gifts of money came our way, the need for space continued to be confirmed, and the Citizens Bank of Swainsboro approved a $30,000 credit line for us. With the final drawing of the plans in hand, we asked for an estimate on the cost. Steve and I had agreed that $60,000 should be our limit for the building, so when the builder said, "You should be able to do this for $60,000, maybe less," we knew the way was clear.

We waited all through Lent for the builder's schedule to open, and on April 14, 1990, Holy Saturday, he came over to study the site. He laid out the parameters of the building with stakes and string, and before he left he hammered a stob with a red flag into the ground, indicating where suppliers were to deliver materials.

A week after Easter Sunday a small group of family and friends gathered with us for a simple ground-breaking ceremony. After we had prayed, sung, "I Love Thy Kingdom, Lord," and read verses from the first chapter of Ephesians, I shoveled up some dirt. Then Steve dug up a spade full, followed by my brother Denny, Steve's father Elick, and my father Woody. We stood on holy ground and turned the earth in deepest respect and gratitude. Work began on the building the very next morning.

April 23, 1990. The builders showed up at 8:00 a.m. sharp. They began laying out the structure of the building that day. I was excited beyond words. In my journal I wrote: "I could have jumped up and down."

On the following Sunday Steve and I took two folding chairs out, placed them on the ground between the strings demarcating rooms, and in the beauty of the late afternoon we prayed Evening Prayer in "the chapel"—accompanied by wind, bugs, setting sun, angels, archangels and all the company of Heaven.

We watched as the grand house grew. It turned into a beautiful building with steep-pitched roof and cedar siding. My grandfather's old tobacco field now held a chapel in its lap, and soon people would be sitting in the quiet of that chapel. "I have calmed and quieted my soul, like a weaned child on the lap of its mother," sang the Psalmist.[2]

By late July the walls were up, the roof was on, and we were ready to return to volunteer help to complete the work. Slowly over the months, with the help of gifted volunteers, we painted, sealed, stained, and prepared the house for use. By the end of January 1991, we were ready to collect furniture—beds, chairs, sofas, desks, tables, bookshelves. Another year would pass before we could afford carpet for the floor, but we could see that if the place was furnished we could begin using it.

Our first guests were my Bolivian baby, now a teenager, and her family who came to spend the night of April 5, 1991. Steve and I were setting up the last bed when they pulled into the driveway. I had last seen Jessica in 1975 when she was three-months old. She would be turning 16 in September, and she wanted to meet me. We had a beautiful reunion. We met on that April evening as if we had never been apart. It seemed fitting that they would be the first to stay here. It was like picking up stitches in some lovely, old piece of embroidery, continuing the pattern that ran through the tapestry. I felt the Retreat House had been duly blessed by the presence of this family.

Soon after this time we began having retreatants stay in the building. Though bare, to be sure, it was also plenty comfortable. Many of these earliest retreatants have stayed connected through the years. It is a joy to have people around who recall those early days and can laugh and wonder and share memories with us.

On November 2, 1992, a beautiful All Saints' afternoon, we dedicated the Retreat House. Joe Way came, and we consecrated every inch of the place with prayer, holy water and incense. Steve and Joe led the liturgy. I told the story of Green Bough and read a few lines from the Song of Songs, evoking the deep prayer of love that speaks of our calling here: "He brought me to the banqueting house, and his intention toward me was love."[3] The Chapel was dedicated to Mary, Mother of God.

The names of our patrons surround the doors of the Chapel, so that all who enter are reminded of those great spirits whose charisms we draw on in our life here. This beautiful border was created by Susan Shaw in 1995. As someone said, "It's like passing through the gates of Heaven." The Chapel is named for Mary Mother of God, and so her name is written above the doors. To the right of her name is Joseph's and to the left is John the Baptist's. Along the left side of the doors are the names of Anthony, Teresa of Avila, Ignatius of Loyola, Therese of Lisieux, and Gandhi. Along the right side are the names of Benedict, Francis of Assisi, Julian of Norwich, Thomas Merton, and Dorothy Day. The names flanking the doors are listed in historical order, top to bottom. We chose these particular saints and witnesses because they support the calling of Green Bough. They were women and men of prayer who sought to live deeply planted in the Spirit, making peace, seeking justice, walking humbly with their God. We depend on their prayer as we live our life together here.

The Houses and the History of Green Bough

The Bell Tower: 1995

In my childhood, church bells still rang to call people to prayer. When I was a little girl my grandmother would lift me up in her arms so that I could catch hold of the rope and ring the bell at the Scott Methodist Church, calling people to come and worship.

One night in June of 1986, while I was still living in Rome, I dreamed about that bell and about my mother; the first time I had dreamed of her since her death. In the dream I heard the bell ringing and went to the church. My Aunt Grace and another person were ringing it. They told me they were getting it ready to use again. I was delighted and asked if I might ring it. I loved the sound. Then I was inside the church in an upstairs room with my mother, who was radiant. She showed me the large windows and how to open them wide, though they had been closed for a long time. The room was bare wood, plain and strangely beautiful. My mother was suggesting that I use it. It was a room for prayer, an upper room, large enough to accommodate several people, even for sleeping. I said, "It is perfect." I asked how people could get to the room, and she showed me the stairs that led to and from it. I felt both excitement and gratitude. My response was, "Yes," which I repeated again and again. My mother was well-pleased.

This is a rich and many-layered dream. Grace was ringing my bell, calling me to prayer, calling me to come up higher, to open windows, to rest in God. It seemed a call to me personally, and it also affirmed my long-held dream of beginning a House of Prayer. The purpose of this new House was a call to a church much in need of being recalled to the upper room and reclaimed for prayer. The Church needed to be re-centered so that it might bear witness to the Spirit which is its very life. Grace is always ringing our bell, inviting us to return to the Center, to consent again to God's activity. Prayer is our way of cooperating.

For years the old bell hung in the Scott Methodist Church, forgotten and unused. After the dream I felt it would one day become a part of this House of Prayer. Soon after we moved to Scott I went to the church to look for the hole in the porch ceiling where a rope once dropped through. I asked Steve to climb into the top of the building to take a look at the bell. When he came down he said, "It's big." When the church had to close its doors I asked for the bell.

The bell now hangs at Green Bough, housed in a bell tower given by my cousin Lynn and her son Michael. The tower was built and dedicated in the autumn of 1995. At the blessing of a church bell the gospel story of Martha and Mary is read—reminding us that the bell rings to call us to "the one thing most needed."[4] It calls us to turn from our busyness, our fretfulness and our fears, and toward the deep awareness that we are in the presence of God.

The Herb of Grace: 1997

The first house I remember living in is the house of my Carter grandparents in Scott. I have loved it through the years. My mother was born in it. She and I lived there in the early 1940s while my father was away at war. A white frame house at the corner of Highway 80 and Pendleton Creek Road, a quarter of a mile from the main Green Bough property, it is graceful in structure and alive with a spirit of love. The light comes smiling through the windows. The front of the house catches the full radiance of morning light, and the back of the house receives the late afternoon glow of sunset. The front porch, with its long swing and two windows of latticework, takes me straight back to my childhood. Our

The Houses and the History of Green Bough

friend Margaret Mathews, a Green Bough Associate (one who vows to live by the Green Bough Rule of Life) and a gifted artist, has chronicled Green Bough in paintings. She did two lovely watercolors of the porch at the Herb of Grace. They hang by my bed where I see them when I go to bed at night and when I rise in the morning.

In 1997, ten years after we came to Green Bough, my Aunt Grace died. She had inherited the house and had been living in it for some years. Once it was vacant, my cousin Hill offered to let us buy it. Although we were not financially able to take him up on the good deal he offered us, my brother Denny stepped in and bought it for Green Bough's use. We rented from Denny, paying whatever we could each month, until the day came when we were able to buy it from him. The house provides sleeping space for five or six people and is a good place for a family to stay. We often use the dining room and kitchen when we have larger groups with us.

The name has an interesting history. After Denny had bought the house I went down to spend some time there. I found a single book lying on a bookcase—a novel called *Pilgrim's Inn* by Elizabeth Goudge. Old monasteries often had a pilgrim's inn where visitors could stay for a short time; the author of this book tells the story of an inn named "Herb of Grace." The herb of grace is the narrow-leaved rue, sometimes used in liturgical settings for sprinkling holy water. In her novel Goudge describes rue as a bitter astringent causing contraction and signifying repentance, compassion, single-mindedness. When you give yourself without reservation, nothing withheld—like a diver committing to a plunge or a person shutting a door behind him that locks itself and prevents his going back—you set your foot on the pilgrim path. Since my aunt's name was Grace it seemed clear that this house should be "The Herb of Grace."

Michael Hryniuk (a doctoral student at Emory) and Ingrid Hauss were our first guests to stay at the Herb of Grace. They filled the space with prayer and hospitality during the year Michael was writing his dissertation.

Joseph's Cottage: 2000

In December 1999, a little cement-block house across the road became available. It had sat vacant all the years we had been here. We shared this news with those gathered at Green Bough to welcome the year 2000. On New Year's Day Mary Alice, one of our board members, came in from a walk saying, "You need to buy that house." After she took up the cause, we placed a prayer in the Chapel at Mary's feet, and by the end of April we had most of the $10,000 we needed to make the purchase. We signed the papers on the morning of May 1. We had not even gone inside the house.

Since the first day of May commemorates the Feast of Joseph the Worker, we wanted to name the house for St. Joseph. In the afternoon we went inside it for the first time. When I saw the condition of the place I was not sure Joseph would consider it an honor to have it named for him. As I wandered through, though, I began to see potential. I could see the beauty of this little house—the layout was good. Sunlight streamed in through the windows, and the space was inviting. It seemed that some scrubbing, some patching here and there, and a few coats of paint could make the place almost nice enough to stay in. We had no need to hurry: we could take our time transforming it.

Our first act was to pray in the place, to warm it for future visitors. One of our Associates (you will learn about Associates soon) was present to pray with us. As she stepped inside, she said in her Australian accent,

Oh, it's a little cawtage." So we named it Joseph's Cottage and set up a small altar with an icon of Joseph, a candle and a vase of flowers. We raised the windows, and with a gentle breeze blowing through the sunny room, we prayed Morning Prayer from the Divine Office. The carpenter of Nazareth, whose name it bears, came to our aid.

Another Associate took on the project of renovating the little house. He organized teams of skilled workers from United Methodist Churches. After assessing the place they stripped it to the studs and started over. Within a few months Joseph's Cottage was brand new—a fitting tribute to Joseph the Worker, whom God chose to care for Mary and Jesus.

Watching the men working faithfully, cheerfully, carefully, day after day, week after week, we came to understand why it is said that "Christ the Lord was honored to be known as the son of a carpenter." Steve, whom I often think of as Joseph, came upon a brick appropriately imprinted: St. Joe. He set it just outside the kitchen door.

The House of Peace: 2003

The House of Peace came next. We had lived for several years with very difficult neighbors. The noise, angry fighting, bad language and loud music were hard to bear. Their household included chickens, goats, a boa constrictor, an occasional pig and always mean dogs. The property was littered with carcasses of old cars, trucks, broken machinery and a couple of ratty trailers people stayed in from time to time. They were dealing illegally in drugs and firearms. It was a busy place. A flag always flew in front of their house—either a Confederate flag or a skull-and-crossbones. One of our Associates said, "You are under surveillance," an idiom meaning that Satan was keeping an eye on Green Bough. We do well to remember that there is a devilish opposition in our world to the Spirit of Love.

A Particle of Light

We made an effort to keep a good relationship with the family. We talked back and forth across the road and often asked them to keep an eye on our property when we were going away. The children in the household had a very hard life, but the silver lining in that cloud was that we were able to give some support to them. They came over regularly for visits, snacks, occasional help with school work, and to use the telephone.

One day one of the children said to me, "Fay, y'all just don't have fun like we do." That was true. This child also said, "Are you all interested in buying our house?" My ears went straight up. "Yes," I said calmly, "whenever you all are ready to sell it." I had never been able to pray for them to move. I believe our neighbors are given to us for a reason. One day at table someone was quizzing me about this, and she said, "Why don't you pray for them to find a better place." I knew I could do that. We asked both our earthly community and the company of heaven to pray with us.

On June 12, 2003, the neighbors called to say they wanted to sell. Steve and I went over to talk with them. They had found a piece of property they liked and wanted to buy. We asked a friend to talk with them about cost. They wanted $38,000, far more than the actual value of the property. However, it was worth it to us. The Board agreed wholeheartedly. We contacted our lawyer, who had helped us throughout the establishing of Green Bough, and on July 2, we bought the house. We had two stipulations: that they vacate the house by August 2, and that they haul off the trailers, the shed, and all the junk strewn around the yard.

For months we worked to get the house ready to use, applying many coats of Kilz and paint, installing new kitchen cabinets and laying new carpet. We asked our longtime friend, Fr. Dennis Berry, to come and oversee the "spiritual cleansing" of the place. He led a small group of us through the house, blessing each room with prayer and holy water. We named it the House of Peace.

Brian Mahan and Kim Boykin, who were staying with us for a couple of years, were the first ones to live in the "new" house. They stayed at the Herb of Grace for several months until we could get the new place ready for them. They were able to move into the House of Peace in December, 2004. Kim's touch turned it into a warm, peaceful space.

A young man named Oliver Ferrari came to live with us in early 2013. Now Oliver lives in the House of Peace, along with his four-legged friend Jolene. He is venturing into organic gardening. I love to watch him as he cares tenderly for the gifts of nature: sowing seeds, nurturing plants, coaxing life of all sorts to nourish us and bring us strength, health and joy. Oliver the Tender—he works with reverence. More will be said about Oliver in the chapter on Community.

The Anchorhold: 2004

One of our Associates kept telling me that I needed some space for myself. She was insistent and set things in motion with a generous gift designated to help build a place for me. This gift became the seed money for a new building. In April 2004, at the beginning of Holy Week, the foundation was set and the framing begun. Work continued steadily through the spring and early summer. The Anchorhold, an irresistible two-room house with cedar siding, tin roof and front porch, took shape.

My hesitancy at moving fell away. It was time for me to move out of the Old House where I had lived for 17 years. Green Bough had grown busier, and my private space had diminished. I needed more privacy, and we needed more space in the Old House for an office. All my years at Hospitality House I stayed in a small cubbyhole, just large enough for a bed and a couple of bookcases. But that was when I was younger. As I grew older my yearning for a space of my own grew stronger. This house was the opening I needed to begin honoring more fully the Anchoress part of my vocation that had long been a part of my calling.

One night, a couple of years before the Anchorhold was built, we were reading from *The Silver Chair*, a volume in C.S. Lewis' *Chronicles of Narnia*. Some words, nineteen of them to be exact, floated through the air, directly into my heart: "a fire of sweet-smelling woods burning on the flat hearth and a lamp hanging from a silver chain…" Something stirred in me. They brought a strong picture of myself sitting in a rocking chair beside such a fire. I was wrapped in a fringed shawl. The words moved through me with illuminating clarity, recalling a line from Rainer Maria Rilke that spoke powerfully to me years ago: "Give birth to your images…. They are the future waiting to be born." This was a prelude to new adventure.

Soon after this experience I received a gift from a friend—a soft, mauve pashmina with fringe on the ends. Mysterious timing. What did it mean? That, like the pashmina, would have to be unfolded. Hearth, fire, solitude, sitting. The image was profoundly alive—and it felt like a call to faithful, ever more faithful prayer, to quiet reflection and a much deeper connection to the Source, to Life, to the Dearest One, to the Fire-at-the-Heart-of-Things. All I could do was say, "Thank You," and wait. It seemed for a moment that the veil had been lifted, and I could see clearly that it was time to begin the turn toward a new stage of my life.

The Houses and the History of Green Bough

I moved from the Old House into the Anchorhold during the week of July 22-29, 2004, a week embraced by the feasts of two saints: Mary Magdalene on the 22nd and Martha on the 29th. I had walked in the company of these two women for years and knew their bracing presence would see me along the rest of my way.

Mary Magdalene, though close to Jesus, did not recognize him after his resurrection. She saw only the gardener until he called her by name. Hearing her name spoken in his familiar voice opened her eyes. Once she *saw*, he entrusted to her the joyful proclamation of resurrection, saying, "Go and tell…" She obeyed. Apostle to the apostles, she announced to them, "I have seen…."[5]

Martha carries the gift of hospitality. Since my mother's name was Martha, this is a special feast day for us at Green Bough. This land on which we live came to us by way of her. Scripture says that Jesus honored Martha by going to her home as a guest. A part of our Green Bough calling is hospitality, serving Christ in our sisters and brothers as we welcome guests here.

It seemed fitting to move during this week. The feasts of these two strong women are like bookends, holding the importance of prayer, solitude and proclamation on the one hand, and on the other a spirit of hospitality and welcome. Slowly over those days we moved my things from the Old House to the Anchorhold, and on the 29th I spent my first night there.

The Anchorhold is situated behind the Old House. Wildflower blue rocking chairs brighten the front porch, and a door-knocker in the shape of an anchor hangs by the door. The anchor is one of the oldest symbols of the Christian tradition. It keeps the ship from drifting with the current. It connects us to bedrock and holds us steady when the weather is wild and the storm threatens. The time had come for me to be an Anchoress.

The Interior of the Chapel of Mary: 2005-2010

The Chapel has always been beautiful, with its high dark ceiling and big windows looking out onto field and sky. Yet the interior was very spare. The room seemed to be waiting for more attention. The Table was front center, with a lectern alongside it for Scripture. These were always dressed in color and symbol, according to church season. Green plants softened the corners of the room. We had several nice pieces of religious art. A Mexican statue of Mary, dark and wearing a deep blue cloak with gold swirls and flowers, her hands folded in prayer stood near the Table. It was given to us by Steve's mother who had received it from a friend. We had an icon of Christ given to us by a friend whose parents brought it back from Turkey in mid-twentieth century. My brother gave us a stained glass window of Jesus in a garden with his arms open in welcome. It came from an old church that was closing, and Denny bought it from the congregation. We hung it in one of the Chapel windows. At the back of the Chapel we set up a small prayer niche with cushions and prayer benches. The big room was lovely but very much in need of something more. It took over fourteen years to find that something more.

The wall that holds the position of Liturgical East in the Chapel was a bare white wall. We wanted a Tree of Life to hang there, but we could never find anything that seemed quite right for the space. Steve and I had come upon the work of Fr. Damian Higgins, an iconographer who had done some pieces for The Oratory in Rock Hill, South Carolina.

The Houses and the History of Green Bough

We happened to be at a conference there when these icons were blessed, and Fr. Damian talked about his work. Both of us liked what we saw and heard. After my father died in July, 2005, memorial gifts to Green Bough made it possible for us to do something special. We agreed that something for the Chapel wall would be a good way to honor him. Steve contacted Fr. Damian and set up a time for us to visit him in Augusta. After spending a morning with him and seeing more of his work, we were ready for him to come to Green Bough, to get a feel for this community. He was agreeable to this. When he visited I told him we wanted a Tree of Life for the wall, and that I wanted him to use some heart pine planks from the floor of my grandfather's tobacco grade house. The three of us talked about colors and images and the vision and general spirit of Green Bough. A few weeks later he returned with a pattern for a very large cross and an outline of his idea for the work. It was to our liking. I knew immediately why we had never seen a piece of art that seemed right for the Chapel wall. We could never have found anything large enough! It needed something made to order, tailored for the particular space. He set to work on the cross, burnishing the hundred year old lumber to a warm gold; then he added the copper flames made by one of his friends in Hawaii. He used rich-colored paints—greens, blues, reds—for leaves and water and circles. By mid-2006 a splendid Tree of Life had emerged.

Now when we enter the Chapel to pray we find ourselves at the foot of the cross "from whence the healing waters flow." The large cross draws us into the wonder of Christ-love, its breadth and length and height and depth, into the compelling heart of Jesus. Along with his work on the walls we also have one of Fr. Damian's icons, Christ the Pantocrator (Ruler of All), given to us by Oliver's mother for the altar table.

I also had asked Fr. Damian to paint a mother pelican with her young over the main doors of the Chapel. In 2008 he began this part of the project. This ancient symbol was assimilated into early Christian imagination, showing up in art on walls and in windows. I first came upon it many years ago in Jerusalem. Legend says that the mother pelican loves her children so dearly that she pierces her breast to feed them with her own blood. A feminine Christ symbol, it is a beautiful rendering of Christ's sacrificial love. Surrounded by the wheat and grapes of the Eucharistic feast, her act of love points to the life-giving compassion of Mother Christ.

Under her wings we can be confident that we are loved, that we will be nourished, our deepest longings satisfied. "In the shadow of your wings we sing for joy," says the Psalmist.[6] Leaving the Chapel we pass under those outstretched wings. Looking up, we see the great costliness of love: we are reminded again that we are invited into that love; that we are called to love one another; that we are called to love God's world; and finally, that we are called to love with God's kind of love.

Then in 2010, Fr. Damian encircled the Chapel with key phrases from the Green Bough Rule of Life. He did this work kneeling on the floor. I watched him. He would kneel, concentrate, assess the words and space, lift his brush, wave it side to side several times like a blessing, and then without hesitation begin the calligraphy. It was beautiful to watch—like seeing prayer being prayed.

My sister-in-law Peggy and friend Daisy helped him with this part of the work, outlining a pattern of lines and interspersing doves. They reminded me of Aaron and Hur holding up the arms of Moses so his hands would be steady as he prayed for the Israelites.

These words, lifted from the Rule and placed on the Chapel walls, are foundational to the Green Bough community. They encompass us as we sit in the Chapel, setting before us daily the work of remembering and anticipating.

The Poustinia: 2015

After Oliver arrived we began expanding the walking trails, taking in the swampy area down in the corner of the field. Oliver was ready to try his hand at building. Steve and I had talked for years about having a small rustic space for prayer in a wooded area. After some talking and dreaming, Oliver, with Steve's help, built a screened-in structure for solitude and prayer, situated along one of the trails. To get to the Poustinia one passes through an archway Oliver made of cedar boughs. Stepping through it is like entering another dimension where time and space seem to shift. A sense of the risk of prayer stirs as one heads to this place for a rendezvous with God. Continuing down the long path and skirting the field's edge, you come upon this treasure tucked in among the trees, just south of the main property. "Let your heart take courage," cries the Psalmist.

The first book I read at the House of Prayer in Rome was Catherine de Hueck Doherty's, *Poustina*, ("pou" pronounced as in "you"). I liked the concept she was presenting. As we played with names this word came to mind. It is the Russian word for desert, but its meaning is richer than that. It points to a place of seclusion and silence where the deepest listening can occur, a place of prayer. In the lonely silence we can meet God in our depths and be made aware once again of our connection with and our responsibility to all. When Jesus invites his disciples to "come away to a lonely place and pray," he is asking them to step out of the noise and busyness of their lives in order to be reminded of their relationship to God and to all that God creates. The Poustinia is the quiet place at the center of the quiet place.

The Sojourner's Cabin: 2017

When we first came to Green Bough, I was envisioning several small hermitages scattered about the property—places where one person could stay for a while, sharing prayer, silence, solitude, meals and brief times of visiting with the community. Steve and I talked about building hermitages, but the early years here necessarily were devoted to other concerns. It took thirty years for this part of the dream to come alive. The first one, aptly named the Sojourner's Cabin, was built in mid-2017. Our Associates and Board encouraged the building of this tiny house. Oliver planned and oversaw the building of it, doing much of the work himself. He explained his idea this way:

> The Sojourner's Cabin is a home for Green Bough sojourners. It is placed at the center of the Green Bough campus to make the sojourners feel themselves supported by the presence and prayer of this community. It is isolated enough to provide a sense of solitude. It is a modest dwelling suitable only for short-term stays.... Its simplicity reminds the sojourner: 'Carry with you only what you need; God alone suffices.'[7]

Our generous Associates largely paid for this structure. An early Associate, Lynnsay Buehler, suggested and oversaw the giving of a gift to underwrite the Sojourner's Cabin. It was presented at Green Bough's 30th anniversary celebration. A sojourner was waiting. An old friend, Nancy Laurel Pettersen, moved in as soon as the space was ready, inaugurating the Cabin with a six-week sabbatical stay.

The Houses and the History of Green Bough

The Main House: Mother Earth

These days I wander slowly around this lovely part of earth and hear God reminding me, "The earth and all that is in it is mine."[8] I am aware that the land houses innumerable life forms, sheltering the great beauty and diversity of God's creation. We have intentionally kept a balance of tended places and wild spaces. As I wander and reflect, the thought comes to me: Green Bough looks *established*.

The land is home to spreading trees where birds nest and sing. Most of the trees were here before we came. Keeping watch through the years, these old trees have faced all weathers. Others we ourselves planted when they were the size of pencils, in the hope that they would one day be tall enough to write upon the sky. Now thirty years later I stand quietly underneath their boughs and can say with the poet Rabindranath Tagore, "Be still my heart; these great trees are prayers."

As the years have passed we have cultivated garden areas with bird feeders, birdbaths, birdhouses, a well-placed chair and table, a bench, a glider given in memory of my cousin Red—places that whisper an invitation to quiet rest, to prayer. Our Associates funded a small pool and fountain, which flows under shadowy pines and provides the calming gurgle of water softly splashing. A memorial garden is developing near the bell tower, enclosed by roses. The ashes of several people are already placed there, marked with inscribed stones. And several others have asked that their ashes be brought to rest here in this place. The labyrinth mown into the field, designed and laid out by our Associate, Lisa Persons, is a favorite place of prayer. People love to walk its winding way, making pilgrimage in all seasons. Walking a labyrinth is an ancient contemplative practice. One walks its circular path, moving always toward the center and then back out again. The path winds in and out, backward and forward, giving one a sense of the circuitous nature of the spiritual journey. The difference between a labyrinth and a maze is that one can get lost in a maze, but the labyrinthine path, though a roundabout way, always moves the walker toward the center and back out. I am reminded of the old Shaker song that includes the words: "To turn, turn will be our delight, 'til by turning, turning, we come round right."

Steve has been the good husbandman who has overseen the development of much of this land, envisioning, planning and caring for these gardens.

Now Oliver joins us, bringing new interests and energy. His love for growing things and his enthusiasm for his work are contagious. He has opened many eyes to the wonders of creation. One day he took us out to see the patch of buckwheat flowering white, right in the middle of the vegetable garden. He dubbed this "the insectiary" since it attracts flying insects of all kinds. Walking along the edge of this area I could see up close butterflies, bees, wasps, dragonflies, moths, ladybugs and numerous little beauties whose names are unknown to me, right along with the common housefly. It may be the only place I ever really have appreciated the wonder of the housefly. As I peered closely at all these tiny creatures manifesting the life force, a wistful memory awakened in me of a time when I was small enough to stand almost eye to eye with these others—delightful, distant little cousins, who are so different from me and yet so close.

The wildness of the unmown field, bearing its own natural beauty, stands in contrast and complement to these cultivated areas. The waving broom sedge, wild plums and blackberries in abundance, weeds and wildflowers of many varieties, provide cover and food for small animals. The field is *home* for rabbits, field mice, birds, snakes, deer, moles, raccoons, spiders…and who knows what else. Mother Earth, the House that houses us all, is given into our care. Wonder and gratitude fill me as my heart affirms: All find their home in You. On your lap sits Green Bough and all its structures and inhabitants.

Chapter 12

Vision

The words vision, prayer, community and service give gentle, yet firm contour to Green Bough. They are the embracing hands which shape and direct the life and work of this House of Prayer. They point to vocation, linking source and ending, interpreting the way of life for us who live here.

Vision comes forth both *from* and *for* the need of a particular time. The longing of our time is for something big enough to challenge the greatness of the human spirit. Though we may not be able to name our yearning, we ache to fall in love with the Mystery at the Heart of Things. The something more we seek is the depth dimension of life, the age-old name of which is God. In *The Divine Milieu*, Teilhard de Chardin wrote: "What I cry out for, like every human being, with my whole life and all my earthly passion is something very different from an equal to cherish: it is a God to adore."[1]

Vision

The Vision of Green Bough

Before Green Bough was founded I was given the overarching vision of it, a vision emerging from years of prayer. The concepts of monastic community; house of prayer; contemplative life; retreat space; spiritual direction; the ordering of the day around set times of prayer; the necessity of both communal and solitary time; the spiritual disciplines that compose our Rule of Life; the need and desire for Associates—all of these were in place before I left Rome. They were given to me through experience, reading and the particular guides who were brought into my life. To create this kind of community the feminine values of relationship, equality, inclusiveness and nurture would need to be honored and supported in a special way. It seems to me that throughout the establishing of Green Bough my task has been to interpret and to find, with Steve's invaluable help, ways to bring the dream into reality.

It was clear to me from the beginning that as a House of Prayer, Green Bough was to be ecumenical: *the household of God*. It was to be a place where people of varied religious and racial backgrounds could come together, a place where seekers and non-believers alike could find welcome. It was to be a bridge where people could meet on equal footing. I thought of it as a place where lines are erased. Though there are many lines that need to disappear, there were three particular ones that I felt we were to address: the division between women and men, the division between laity and clergy, and the division among denominations or even religions (though we clearly, unapologetically are Christian). The lines of separation were to disappear at Green Bough. I am very sure that these lines were never drawn by God—only by humans. Prayer is a place of meeting. We sit at a round table, in the presence of the One who made us all, with no walls between us.

I also knew that whatever Green Bough was to become it needed to start small, and it should not be concerned with growing fast or becoming big. Jesus tells us of the tiny mustard seed that grows slowly, organically into a tree that becomes a place of nesting and shelter.[2] And then, there is the story of Jesus taking the gift of a few loaves and a couple of fish and to the wonder of all, multiplying that small offering to feed thousands. This story, told six times in the four Gospels, gives us the divine pattern: God's presence, our trust, God's action. I bow before the One who takes the small and makes it enough-and-to-spare, who takes the insignificant and imbues it with meaning and purpose.

This vision emerged from a larger context. In 1986 as I was leaving Rome, I told friends I was going to take monasticism to middle Georgia. One replied, "You are going into the desert!" I said, "It's time for the desert to bloom." I love to think of a new flowering of monasticism in the deserts of the world. We live in a secular age and can see around us the breaking down of institutions that have carried the weight of our faith for hundreds of years and are now worn out. An old concept reinterpreted for a new day could become a sign of possibility amid the ruins. Monasticism could again perform one of its early functions—protecting culture when it is under assault and preserving the spiritual treasure of Church in a time when deep tradition might easily be lost or left behind. It has been said that there are times when battleships sink and corks float. Small monastic communities can be the floating corks that carry the treasure of the ages until new institutions can emerge.

We live on the cusp of death and life, standing with one foot in an age that is dying and one foot in an age yet to be born. As we straddle the gap we face two temptations: fear and arrogance. Fear shuts down our capacity to be open to the new, causing us to lock the doors, pull down the blinds and cling defensively to what is passing away. Arrogance seduces us into turning our backs on the past, dismissing tradition and wisdom, and rushing forward without discernment. The monk's task is to live the tension between the old and the new. In the quiet heart contradictions are resolved. We can freely ask, "What do you want, God?" We listen for clarity—then we act wholeheartedly.

It seems to me that the specific task of our time, the soul-sized task of every small monastic community, is to stand in the rubble and dream. We must stand peering into the reality of what *is* until we glimpse the ancient vision, without which the people perish.[3] Then our own dream for the future can take on shape and substance, and we can sing a *new* song to God. The monk cries out: "My heart is ready, O God, my heart is ready!" And though we do not know what it means for us, we take the Psalmist's words as ours: "I will sing and make melody. Awake, my soul! I will awake the dawn."[4] I think of Green Bough as one of those places to stand, dream, envision and sing the new song. Such a community calls forth and supports the intentional living-out of one's God-given responsibility to join in the work of awaking the dawn.

In its origins monasticism was a lay movement, drawing men and women whose hearts yearned for the "more" of the Gospel. Today hope lies in small, vowed monastic communities of people called to live the contemplative life. The work of small faith communities will be to roll up our sleeves and reach far, far back into the deepest memory of our faith history. (I would also include here individuals who live as "monks in the world"—people who are awake, reflective, compassionate, visionary.)

One of the foundational stories of our faith tells of Moses leading the Israelites out of slavery and into freedom. This is the story of each human soul as well as our corporate faith story. "Moses took with him the bones of Joseph who had required a solemn oath of the Israelites, saying, 'God will surely take notice of you, and then you must carry my bones with you from here.'"⁵ The ancient gifts of wisdom and tradition are invaluable, and we must carry them with us as we are led toward freedom and new life. The bones of Joseph! The essentials of our faith: first, God's unconditional, steadfast love; and second, God's intention to bring us forth from bondage—from any Pharaoh that would enslave us, any death that would keep us from life. When we have lived too long bound by anything, like it or not, God will take notice. In love God seeks us out, wherever we are, and calls us to freedom.

The bones of our deep tradition provide structure for a new life where we can stand together, without the petty things that keep us divided from ourselves, one another and God. We must shake off any clinging dirt, decayed muscle or sinew—attitudes, habits, prejudices, fears—and grow new flesh on old bones. God, whose hand is mightier than the hand of Pharaoh, will come to our aid.

Living toward this vision is our daily work. Step by step we move along, toward the land we will be shown, usually some as-yet-unexplored interior space, perhaps a place of darkness and light, where the height and depth and breadth of the human spirit might stretch our hearts to the full. We live by faith, venturing all, committing ourselves to the unknown, uncertain future, with all its threat and promise. Love sets us on this way, and Love accompanies us.

Perhaps another name for this vision is Reign of God. A friend brought me Martin Buber's description of the Kingdom of God. He says it is "the kingdom of danger and of risk, of eternal beginning and of eternal becoming, of opened spirit and deep realization, the kingdom of holy insecurity"⁶ The resonance of truth strikes deep and makes me long to be bold. This path into God is *adventure*, with all the risk and reverence that entails.

Chapter 13

Prayer

God, who creates us and loves us, invites us into relationship. Prayer is our response to that invitation. In a world that can trap us in the distraction of noise and isolate us with busyness, a discipline of prayer helps us focus on the *reality of God*. We belong to God; all our moments belong to God. A habit of prayer keeps us growing in awareness and gratitude. We come to trust that our tears, laughter, struggles, service, work, play, love, giving, receiving—all are consecrated by prayer.

The Daily Round

Prayer is at the center of our life together. From the beginning of Green Bough our days have been framed with prayer. Acknowledging that our times belong to God, Steve and I set up a small altar in the living room of the Old House and established a daily rhythm of prayer—a pattern that continues today. As a community we gather for Morning Prayer, Evening Prayer and Night Prayer from the *Liturgy of the Hours*.

Along with corporate prayer we find time each day for personal prayer, when we are attentive to the steady, patient, laboring of God in us. We live in the presence of God, and God asks us to *be present* in our daily living, open to encountering the Divine in every moment, happening and circumstance. The Church has given us a great tool for structuring our daily prayer: *The Divine Office*, also known as the *Liturgy of the Hours*. This liturgical prayer has been the central expression of Christian community since the early days of the Church, enabling communities to pray both with the Church and on behalf of it.

The Divine Office: The Liturgy of the Hours

The Divine Office anchors our days and binds us with the People of God through time and space. It links our prayer with the prayer of those gone before us and those to come after us. And it joins us with communities and individuals around our tiny, spinning planet, as we take our turn in the round of prayer for all God's creation. While others sleep we take up the task. When we sleep, others are praying. In this company we enter into the ongoing prayer of Christ.

This *Liturgy of the Hours* is based on a four-week cycle. Over and over we pray the antiphons, Psalms, and prayers appointed for the day. The antiphons are short verses of Scripture that introduce the central thought of each Psalm. They change through the year, filtering the Psalm's meaning through the lens of the particular season—Advent, Christmas, Epiphany; Lent, Easter, Pentecost, and the long periods of Ordinary Time that carry the bulk of the year. Feast Days (also having special antiphons) fall in place year after year. As we circle through this order over time something is formed in us—a sense of being in God's presence at all times. We begin to see, hear, taste, touch, catch the very scent of God, moment by moment, day by day.

Sometimes people ask, "Isn't it boring going over the same stuff every four weeks?" The truth is that we are at a different place each time, discovering a nuance not seen before. Just as the sunlight changes through the seasons of the year, the angle of light shines differently on the Office as we go through the liturgical cycle casting a different light on the readings. The repetition is a gift, spiraling us deeper each time around.

The Psalms are the prayers of the people of God. Jesus himself prayed them. They teach us honesty before God, enabling us to express the range of human emotions and moods—from anger to praise, defeat to triumph, weariness to wonder, sorrow to joy. The words and phrases of Scripture are gradually kneaded into us. They take hold and rise into our consciousness as we need them, giving name and direction to the experiences of our days.

After praying the Office we sit in silence, open, listening, ready to receive and appropriate God's Word for our given day and situation. This is the ongoing pattern of our corporate prayer here at Green Bough.

Taking Up and Laying Down: Intercession and Compline

Intercessory prayer is a special part of our work. We keep an intercession book by the Chapel door for people to write down prayer requests and concerns. Daily we hold in God's healing Light the widening circle of family, neighbor, world. Our Rule reminds us to "call to mind each day the plight of the poor and the needs of the world's peoples." We gather into our hearts the suffering of the world, all who live with violence and war; refugees and immigrants cut off from family and homeland; those who struggle for freedom and justice. We pray for oppressors as well as oppressed, for the leaders of nations and all who wield power. We pray for the earth itself and all its creatures—and for our own needs here at Green Bough. Wherever there is division the healing work of intercession is called for.

To intercede is to stand between heaven and earth, crying out to God on behalf of the suffering world and crying out to the suffering world on behalf of God. As we look deep into the darkness and divisions of our time we are carried by the wind of promises from old prophets. They tell of God's vision for the world, and we take up their cry, "On that day…" this is how it will be: enemies will embrace and opposites sit down together; children will play in safety; war will be studied no more and swords and spears will be hammered into garden tools; we will sit unafraid under our vines and fig trees and invite one another into the peace and plenty; tears will be dried; sorrow and sighing will be no more; every head will be crowned with everlasting joy. This is God's dream for the world. We must plant it deep. It lies for now in the realm of the not yet, and so we cry out to God for help, staking our lives on the promise that all is possible.

That means for us IMAGINING the world as the prophets have seen it. Our imagining is our way of crying out to God on behalf of creation for the healing of division. We imagine it interiorly in the universe of the self. We imagine it outwardly in family and neighborhood; in individuals, nations, systems and structures. We imagine it out to the far reaches of the spacious, starry universe. That is our work, the work we take up in intercession.

Then there is the hard prayer that Jesus expects of us—we pray for our enemies. Jesus insists on this prayer because it is transforming prayer. It works its work *in us*. It is truly Jesus praying in us, because it is prayer we alone cannot pray. It may or may not change the enemy. But it most certainly changes us, taking us directly to the place where we come to know that *we are one*—with Christ, with ourselves, with each other. It is the place where the Cross becomes the Tree of Life, where Love manifests itself radically. As we pray for the enemy, whether it is inside us or outside us (and I would say that our most dangerous and destructive enemies are always inside us—enemies such as fear, anger, shame, despair), we stumble upon the truth that in Christ every two is made one.[1] Whenever we go into our Chapel and sit before the great Tree of Life there we are reminded of this.

Our days end with *Night Prayer*, a time for reflecting, letting go, trusting. In grateful awareness of God's steadfast love, we confess and lay aside the ups and downs of the day. Each night we pray the words of Simeon when he sees the Christ-Child in the temple, "Now you let your servant go in peace for I have seen your salvation…."[2] As we wait in the quiet, with the glow of candles and the smell of incense filling the Chapel, those words bless the whole day. What we may have missed in our busyness, we come to see in this still moment: God is with us—has been with us throughout the day—revealing salvation in each moment. Life itself is the temple where Christ is ever present. The Church has named this night office Compline, which means *complete*. The day is over. It is time to rest. We are held in the eternal love of God.

Eucharist: Table Prayer

The Table at the heart of our faith stretches through space and time. Jesus, our Bread of Life, was born in a stable and cradled in the feeding trough of animals. We gather at the Eucharistic Table to give thanks for the gift of Christ, to be fed Christ and to offer ourselves to be taken up into the healing work of Christ. We proclaim: *Christ has died. Christ is risen. Christ will come again.* At this table of thanksgiving we say, "Let us receive You; let us be You, for one another, for your world." When we look through the broken bread into the face of another, we see that person differently. When we look through the chalice into the face of another, we see not only one for whom Christ's life was broken and spilled out, *we see Christ*. Bread broken, wine poured—the agency of God. And if we look through the eyes of faith, we see across the Table those gone before us, gathered and present with us.

We believe that every meal is a celebration of the Feast, with Christ as both Host and Guest. The Bread of Life is also on our kitchen table. Our Rule reminds us that "we celebrate the hope of Christ each day as we gather at table, making each meal a remembrance of Christ's feast."

I have just returned from Morning Prayer. The brisk air has called me to attention, the chill of shadows giving way to bright, sunlit patches that warm the earth and me like joy. As I reach the steps of the Anchorhold I turn and suddenly see the Chinese tallow tree aflame in gold and red—a burning bush. The beauty melts me. I have stood under that tree many autumns, letting its golden glow envelop me. I am aware. I am alive. I stand on holy ground rooted and grounded in the Love that is the ground of all—and I know it. The world is full of Light. God has said, "Here I am." My prayer: Thank You. Thank You. Thank You. Is there any other appropriate response? If only I could give this moment away, to everyone, everywhere. If only everyone everywhere could experience such a call to love on a bright November morning.

Prayer

I know that I cannot give this moment to anyone. As human beings we do not hold that power. We can, however, live in a way that points to God's presence among us and in us. We can provide a place where prayer is ongoing, where quietness, stillness, beauty, slow pace, call attention to the One who is at the heart of things. That is what we can do. This little community, in its life together, is a sign of God's presence, pointing to the Love that enfolds and fills all creation, to the Light shining in the darkness. How does one live into depth and richness and meaning? I like to think that Green Bough, (and other small intentional communities), offers a pattern for just such a life of awareness and wonder.

Chapter 14

COMMUNITY

The word *religion* comes from a Latin word meaning to re-connect, to tie together again. Mobility, technology and isolation have weakened the bonds of community, leading to an epidemic of loneliness and anxiety throughout our culture. There is an acute need for community, where love, care and support enrich daily life. How do we reweave ties that can bind us in healthy relationship, in bonds of love that hold us together? This is a Spirit question.

Forming Community: Bonds of Christian Love

In some ways those of us who live at Green Bough are creating the road as we walk it. There are few models for what we are doing. There are, of course, the gifts of old communities and the wisdom of the ages but they must be reinterpreted for our time. We are called to be what the world needs at this time—a sign of Jesus' love lived out as contemplative religious community. We are thirty years into this venture. Living by a Rule of Life, an old monastic practice, gives pattern to our days.

Community

Living by the Rule

The Rule holds us to the truth that *we live in the presence of God*. It functions as both reminder and sign. As St. Ignatius put it: "We come from God. We belong to God. We go to God." *The whole of life is set in God*. As forgetful people we need reminding of this. The Rule is a tool for helping us remember who we are. It also functions to enable our life together to be sign and witness in the world. The great task of our contemplative vocation is to *be reminder* of this for our contemporary, busy, secular world, and, truth be told, for the church.

The Rule determines the daily round of our life together—our prayer, work, leisure, solitary time, community time. In church tradition a Rule of Life has been understood as a *trellis* on which the spiritual life might grow in an ordered way. One of our early Associates said, "I need a trellis for the kudzu of my life." We all do, though we may not know it. It is easy to get lost in a haphazard, casual way of living. A framework of good habits can be a great help. An ordered round for the day enables us to live with more awareness, attentiveness and intention. *The Rule in no way affects God's love for us*. Rather, it *enables us to love God more fully*. God does not love more or less. God simply loves. God is love. The Rule helps us respond out of a grateful heart to the Love that calls, "Come to me…that you may live." Most simply we can say that Christ is our Rule of Life—our measure, our mirror, our way.

While Green Bough was still a dream I wrote down seven disciplines that I thought should be a part of a Rule of Life for the community. They were: the sacrament of the present moment, prayer, simplicity, silence and solitude, spiritual direction, spiritual reading, and Eucharist. They were disciplines that had been helpful in guiding my own days for several years. I knew if we were going to be a true community we would need a Rule of Life. We could not have novices, associates and affiliates without a Rule. When Steve and I came to Scott I shared these disciplines with him. The two of us lived by them for a couple of years to see if they seemed right for this new venture in contemplative community.

Meantime, we read Rules: *The Rule of the Master, The Rule of St. Benedict, The Rule of Taize, Rule for a New Brother, The Jerusalem Rule.* They were good spiritual reading, and we gained much by reflecting on them. I also was moved by the short personal *Rule of Life* that Raissa Maritain had written in 1923 for the three members of her household—herself, her husband Jacques and her sister Vera.[1]

After two years of living in discernment with these seven classical disciplines, it became plain that they were appropriate for our life together here. It was time for us to write out our Rule, and we wanted to do that in a setting of monastic prayer. Steve and I made three trips to the Monastery of the Holy Spirit in Conyers, Georgia, to write. On the first two visits we wrote out the entire Rule. We worked until we felt we had something simple and sturdy enough to help us grow in love of God and neighbor, to help us live out our faith intentionally day by day. We then took it to Joe Way to edit. He made a few good suggestions, and on the third trip we rewrote and refined the Rule. Joe approved it so by late 1990 we were ready to make it available for others.

The Rule takes into account the two things necessary in the spiritual life: love of God and love of neighbor, devotion and service. It ends with the reminder that it is here, now, *in the present moment* that we encounter God, that we love, adore, worship God—and we do that "with angels, archangels and all the company of Heaven." This sets our particularity within the context of the universal, taking our own small and very ordinary lives into the Community of the Trinity. (A copy of our Rule is included under Postlude.)

The Community of the Table

The kitchen was the first room made ready at Green Bough. It was a sign for me that all would be well. Once it was painted and the flooring laid I knew for certain that the dream of Green Bough would become reality. I knew that I not only could live in the Old House, but that I also wanted to live in it. I gathered some wild flowers and put them in a small vase on the mantel. Then I placed a small plaque bearing the word SHALOM alongside the flowers. It was the Mother's blessing. The plaque had belonged to my mother. It now hangs by the front door of the Retreat House. Over the years the kitchen with its aromas and bustle has held a central place in the community. Steve and I worked together to create an aura of goodness and welcome there.

As my work as a spiritual director grew, I began to move out of the kitchen—except for making communion bread, which I love to do, and occasional desserts. Steve's gifts with food emerged. He has a good eye for recipes and prepares our fare to perfection. He fills the table again and again with meals both simple and rich. He has brought his love and creativity to the table, making it a place of feasting and joy. Under his care the humble old kitchen magically becomes a banqueting room, giving us a foretaste of Heaven. Our Rule reminds us that "each meal is a remembrance of Christ's feast." I am content to do the dishes.

And now, of course, there is Oliver Ferrari who has brought a new level of interest to the table. His organic garden provides a colorful harvest of vegetables and melons, keeping us aware of the mystery and power of a seed. He has a flock of chickens that provide eggs, and he has begun working on an orchard that will give us fruits and berries. The harvest is abundant enough to occasionally offer a Kitchen Table Farmer's Market to retreatants as they leave.

The round oak table that sits in the Green Bough kitchen is over 100 years old. It belonged to my Carter grandparents and resided for many years in the dining room at what is now the Herb of Grace. In the warmth of its wood memories are stored, blessing held. It seems alive with remembrance of gracious meals and happy gatherings of another era. After a retirement of many years, it was brought back into service in 1987, and for these last 30 years it has been at Green Bough, expanding and contracting as is needed. More people than we can count have sat at this table over the years—gathered for a meal enjoyed in silence or, from time to time, engaging in the gift of good conversation and the sharing of stories.

After our meals we have a reading—an old monastic practice. At lunch we read from Robert Ellsberg's *All Saints*, a book of short biographical reflections on people who are witnesses to God's love. These pieces are variations on the theme of God's mighty acts performed in, for and through people. We are fed with the nourishing bread of these lives and feel the blessedness of being surrounded by a great cloud of witnesses. As we hear these stories of faith, challenge, sweetness, danger, suffering and risk, we pass around a plate of chocolates. I often say we serve chocolates with our saints so that when "our time" comes we will associate it with something sweet. Our friend Brian Mahan once said, "Yes, when they take me before the firing squad I'll say, 'Oh, I don't need a blindfold. Just give me a York Pattie.'"

Our reading following evening meals is usually poetry, essay or fiction, something that invites reflection. We read all kinds of things: poems by Mary Oliver, Naomi Shihab Nye, Anne Porter, Rilke, Hafiz or Rumi; also both poetry and novels by Wendell Berry; C.S. Lewis' *Chronicles of Narnia*, book by book, a chapter a night; George McDonald's *The Golden Key*; and sometimes an essay from Reynolds Price's *Feasting the Heart*. A good reading along with dessert makes the whole meal more delicious.

A Table is the centerpiece of the community of faith. Jesus enjoyed good meals at the homes of his friends. He also provided a few himself. And along our way, as people of faith, we catch a glimpse of "something more." We anticipate what we long for—the great end-time Banquet when ALL will be gathered for the feast. The whole family of creation will be gathered at the Table. That is worth imagining—imagining into reality. I raise a glass to the community of love: Vive la Compagnie!

Community: Seed Gathered and Scattered

Green Bough has grown steadily, from seed to flower to fruit. At first, only Steve and I were here, planted like two seeds in an out-of-the-way corner of a garden. We were the gathered community of Green Bough, gathered to pray. A part of our prayer from the beginning was that God would bring people here who needed to come and people we needed to have come. Slowly over the years the community has expanded beyond its local, gathered manifestation into a widely scattered community of people committed to living as contemplatives. Seed sown by a strong and generous Hand! We have imagined Green Bough as a *growing* community, offering several options for people who want to be related to us here. We use the language of traditional religious communities for these categories of relationship. They are: Professed Resident Members, Novices, Associates and Affiliates.

Affiliates: Affiliates have a special relationship with the Green Bough community. They live and work elsewhere, but occasionally spend longer periods of time at Green Bough. They are committed to live by the Rule, and they participate in the life of the community when in residence. Affiliates also may live at or near Green Bough, participating in the community life but without becoming professed members.

Associates: Traditionally there is a provision in religious life that offers non-residents a way to be committed to a monastic community, by becoming Oblates or Associates. Our Associates are people who have come to Green Bough for several years, making retreat and getting acquainted with the life of contemplative community. They find themselves drawn to a deeper experience of spiritual life and a commitment to live contemplatively. Becoming an Associate is a way of entering into a formal relationship with this community without becoming a resident. After praying with the Green Bough Rule of Life over a period of time, reflecting on how they can live it in their own settings, interpreting it for their own particular lives they take a vow to live accountable to the Rule, to pray for the community and to make a yearly retreat at Green Bough.

Novices: Novices live as resident interns with the community for at least a year before covenanting to move into the novitiate process. The novice takes a vow, renewed annually for five years giving the aspirant a long period to discern whether he or she wants to stay on as a Professed Resident Member. Novices live by the Green Bough Rule of Life and are faithful to the traditional vows of religious life: poverty, chastity and obedience. They meet with Professed Members for spiritual direction and mentoring. At the end of the novitiate the resident community and the novice together discern whether or not the novice is called to take full vows.

Professed Resident Members: By mutual consent of the novice and the community a person may become a Professed Resident Member, establishing stable residency at Green Bough, living by the Rule and taking vows of poverty, chastity and obedience. Residents are the heart of the contemplative calling of this community.

The People of the Green Bough Community

Professed Resident Members: Steve and I were the founding members. We made our vows of poverty, chastity and obedience on January 25, 1992, in our fifth year at Green Bough. We each wear a ring inscribed with the words, THOU ALONE. We both happen to be United Methodist, Steve as clergy, I as layperson. I must in all honesty say that I have a Catholic heart in my Methodist body, finding myself on the border, living where God seems to want me. People sometimes ask why I have not become Catholic, and all I can say is that I have not felt God asking that of me. Perhaps I am needed more as a bridge across divides.

Novices: Several wonderful people have "tried on" the contemplative life here, with an interest in becoming resident members of the community. They are people I love and admire greatly, people through whom God is working in rich and vital ways in other places. Daily I pray for them by name. For various reasons they did not stay long term at Green Bough. I had much to learn about working new people into the ongoing life of community and am clear that often I failed to guide the transitions well. I also know that calling is couched in mystery, and much cannot be explained rationally.

Oliver Ferrari moved to Green Bough on January 6, 2013. He came to pray. After visiting several times he asked about staying for six months to explore the possibility of life as a monastic. He seemed a good fit from the very first moment. When he arrived in the late afternoon of Epiphany, Steve met him and brought him to the Anchorhold. After warm greetings the three of us prayed the Lord's Prayer together, and I suggested he pray with the story of the Wise Men, from the second chapter of the Gospel of Matthew, considering that his entry into life at Green Bough is his way of kneeling before the Christ Child, opening his treasure chest and offering Him his gifts.

Over a year later, October 4, 2014, Feast of St. Francis of Assisi, Oliver became a Novice here, in a simple, reverent ceremony. He knocked on the Chapel Door, and we asked who was knocking. He gave his name, and we asked why he wanted to come in. He responded, "For love of God." We opened wide the doors and read from Leviticus 23:10: "When you enter the land that I am giving you and you reap its harvest, you shall bring the sheaf of the first fruits of your harvest to the altar."[2] We invited Oliver into this house, and he entered carrying a basket with several things in it symbolizing the particular gifts he felt he was bringing. After placing the basket at Mary's feet he knelt before the altar and vowed to give himself "wholeheartedly to these years of service, formation, prayer and discernment." He then prayed a prayer of his own composition: "To this community, to Christ, I offer what God has given me, my body, heart, mind and spirit, symbolized in these items. In deep gratitude for this place and this community, I ask for the grace to journey onward and to be present to others on their journeys." With great joy Steve and I welcomed him, receiving him as a Novice of Green Bough and pledging him our prayer.

A few months after Oliver came to Green Bough his mother, Lalor, gave me a beautiful statue of St. Francis. It sits on the porch of the Anchorhold.

Community

She had no idea at the time that Oliver would become a Novice here. It seems one of God's sweet gifts that Oliver should have chosen the Feast of St. Francis to make his vows. When he renews his vow each year we place the statue in the Chapel for the celebration. And we read from Robert Ellsberg's biographical piece on St. Francis in his book *All Saints*:

> Francis had a vivid sense of the sacramentality of creation. All things, whether living or inanimate, reflected their Creator's love and were thus due reverence and wonder. In this spirit he composed his famous "Canticle of Creation," singing the praises of Brother Sun, Sister Moon, and even Sister Death. Altogether his life and his relationship with the world—including animals, the elements, the poor and sick, as well as princes and prelates, women as well as men, represented the breakthrough of a new model of human and cosmic community.[3]

Words so apt for the occasion I am certain the Saint pokes Oliver with his elbow when they are read.

Affiliates: On July 27, 2007, Brian Mahan and Kim Boykin became Affiliates of Green Bough as we sent them out from three years of life here. One year they lived here part-time, the next two mostly fulltime. They wanted to establish formal ties with the community before they left. In a simple ceremony we sent them out as Affiliates of Green Bough, with the charge to carry the charism of this community as they moved into the next phase of their lives. They continue to visit when they can, and Brian writes an annual Affiliate's Report to the community.

Associates: After we had written the Rule of Life and Steve and I had made our vows, we opened the door to receiving Associates as a part of the community. Margaret Bullington, Steve's mother, became our first

Associate, taking her vow on March 4, 1992. Slowly over the years people have asked about this relationship, expressing a desire to be more deeply connected to Green Bough. Now we have over 70 Associates, amazing people strongly committed to prayer. They are contemplatives living in many different settings, scattered as far away as California and Canada. They enlarge the life of Green Bough, sowing the seed of prayer far and wide. We pray together, for one another and for our world. They support this community in countless ways.

Retreatants: Retreatants have a faithful though not formal connection to Green Bough. Retreat is where it all begins. Without retreatants there would be no formal categories of relationship to the Green Bough community. The hundreds and hundreds of people who have come on retreat over the years are an important part of this community, whether or not they have established a formal connection. Many have come dozens of times, often saying, "I want to take the spirit of this place with me into my daily life." Seed of God's sowing, scattered around the world, these retreatants are among our beloveds, and we are thankful for them and their ongoing connection to Green Bough.

Dreaming of Growing: The Future

We dream of growing and hope that the gathered community will increase. We pray that some will desire to live the vowed life, holding the heart of Green Bough's beginning vision and witness. The word *charism* is used in religious life to denote a gift of power and authority bestowed by God. The charism of a religious community is the gift of a particular calling and purpose to be used in the service of God. The charism of Green Bough is the holding of prayer and spiritual life as the very heart of the life of faith. Without its vowed center I am not sure that Green

Bough could be faithful to the charism it was given. With a small vowed group of Professed Resident Members at its heart Green Bough can be a strong magnet for others to live nearby, in a variety of relationships with the community. A stable contemplative center can make *life together* possible.

The year 2017 brought us a sign of growth. Holly Book, one of our Associates, and her husband Bob have bought a house here, which they have named "Heartsong." This came about when Holly telephoned to re-schedule a retreat date. Before hanging up, Steve mentioned that the house down the road, built by Gail Pitt some years back, had recently come up for sale, and we were asking our Associates to pray with us about Green Bough's response to that. Early the next morning Holly called back, saying, "Why don't I buy that house?" She had been wanting to spend more time at Green Bough. Within a couple of weeks the entire process was completed. She will be staying at Green Bough part-time, praying with the community, sharing occasional meals and community activities and entering into a more solitary kind of life. Her husband Bob, an Episcopal priest who is semi-retired, will be coming and going here as well. This has set us wondering and hoping. What might Holly and Bob's presence mean for this community? Where will this new growing take us? We are open.

The Gift of Community: A Labor of Love

In religious life it is said that two *charisms* (God-bestowed gifts) are given when something new is called into being. The first is the "founding charism," the second is the "supporting charism," given to confirm the first. The founder is given the vision and must lay it out with clarity, conviction and forceful energy while issuing an invitation to pioneer new territory. The one who is given the supporting charism brings steadiness and patience to the task, enabling the vision to move forward, making it work. Both are necessary, one complementing the other. This relationship requires a strong commitment—to God, to the vision given and to one another. It is hard to bring a dream into reality.

In truth nothing gets born and nothing grows without struggle and pain. I knew that what God expected of me here was *faithfulness*, nothing more, nothing less. The work of God is creating, bringing to birth—and God asks us to co-create with Him. If we say yes the Spirit moves in, the power of the Most High overshadows and what is born will be called holy.[4] Nothing is ever said about this being an easy labor. I knew it would be hard. YES was my answer—with only occasional doubts and waffling.

Steve is the beautiful person God sent to confirm my calling to start Green Bough. I love this man of prayer whom God sent bringing the very gifts needed to complement mine. Steve has given devoted support to this dream. He has prayed and made music. He has tended the land and cared for details. He has cultivated the beauty of the grounds. And he has brought his God-given beauty to his service at the Eucharistic Table and the kitchen table—which finally are one and the same. His faithfulness and hard work on behalf of Green Bough have made it grow. My heartfelt thanks for him knows no bounds.

As I have indicated earlier there can be no community without conflict. This is true of *every community*. Jesus says, "Where two or three are gathered in my name, I am there."[5] Perhaps Christ is sometimes spelled C-o-n-f-l-i-c-t, sometimes C-o-m-p-r-o-m-i-s-e. One of the gifts of the years has been learning to work *together* for the common good.

We have had to review the vision from time to time, redirecting it to something more suitable for both of us, finding ways to compromise without sacrificing integrity. In our Rule we speak of "the rub of community life" as a part of the Sacrament of the Present Moment, the very place where Christ is made known to us. Indeed, it is the give-and-take of daily life that teaches us *how to be* community. The great learning is around *life together*. In an age when long-term commitment is held in low esteem, this is an important learning. Steve is the one whose hands I have held firmly over the years, even when we have pulled against one another. He keeps me humble—a part of his job. We have always managed to work things through, finding our passage across the rough waters. Forgiveness and grace are ever active. We have had laughter and sweetness aplenty. I can say without hesitation that this life is good! The stars shine on us at night and give us a wink of blessing.

I once dreamed I was standing on the back porch of the Old House. It was night, and there was a light shining in the sky. I lifted my hands and leaped up, and my hands became sparks of light, like dancing stars. I was amazed and cried out to Steve, "Do you see? Do you see the stars?" He was standing in the field behind the house and responded by holding his hands high and jumping up. His hands too sparkled with light. We played, swapping places from field to house and back again, and I kept crying out, "Do you see? Do you see the stars?" I awoke feeling full of light and joy.

No Journey without Temptations

Naturally, temptations to bolt arise from time to time. Once some years ago I had reached a terrible point of conflict. Fears and doubts about my ability to oversee Green Bough had risen in me like threatening specters.

I doubted whether the community would or could grow if I stayed. I began to wonder if I should leave. I received a resounding "No!" to such a thought. Steve and I were visiting my friend Betty in Pittsburgh. I always love going to the National Aviary there, and so the three of us spent a morning looking at birds. I had wandered off by myself down a narrow path, and something caught my eye. I stopped to look more closely and saw a white peacock, tail folded, standing quietly under a tree. I stood still too, looking at him. Our eyes engaged, and he came toward me. As we stood before one another he suddenly spread his tail and the full glory of white feathers shimmering there stunned me. I spread my arms wide before him, and we greeted one another in this way for a long time. Finally I went to find Betty and Steve so they could see this glorious bird. By the time we got back to him, he was standing quietly, tail folded, under the tree, and did not move from there. As we returned to Betty's house, I stepped out of the car, and there at my foot was one single pigeon feather. The thought came to me: *Seeing this one feather is like receiving a peck on the cheek after a passionate embrace.* I went upstairs to the room where I was staying, and beside my bed was a book called *Dear Heart, Come Home*, by Joyce Rupp. I picked it up and let it fall open. Words about a Native American creation myth were at my fingertips: "…whenever two-legged creatures are on their spiritual path, following their passion, they will find a feather on their path."6 I ran back downstairs and out the front door to pick up the pigeon feather. I have it still, tucked behind a small cross in my room, as reminder of God's way of saying loudly: YOU ARE ON THE RIGHT PATH. YOU ARE WHERE YOU NEED TO BE. An Associate gave me a picture of a white peacock with its tail fully spread. I keep it on the kitchen mantel as reminder. All along a feather lies in my path, a tether to reality: "It is HERE God gives me my place among all the faithful" (Green Bough Rule of Life).

Community

My personal struggle, I think, will ever be to *try not to take up too much space and still be myself.* Several years ago a good friend gave me a beautiful picture of a crane with its wings fully spread. My heart aches with longing as I look at it. It sets before me the work of ongoing discernment: knowing when to spread my wings and when to keep them folded. I long to be attentive and acquiescent to the Spirit's guidance.

"Trust," my heart says over and over. Trust in your God. The way is not easy, but God is faithful. Jeremiah assures us:

> Blessed are those who trust in the Lord,
> > whose trust is the Lord.
> They shall be like a tree planted by water,
> > sending out its roots by the stream.
> It shall not fear when heat comes,
> > and its leaves shall stay green;
> In the year of drought it is not anxious
> > and it does not cease to bear fruit.[7]

What I cannot do well, or cannot do at all, does not matter. I belong to Another whose love covers all and accomplishes all, and makes much of my small gift of self.

Chapter 15

SERVICE

Green Bough was called into being as a small contemplative community. In today's church we see an acceptance of and adaptation to the rationalism, individualism and materialism pervading our culture and world. Religious communities often come into being to redress a particular weakness in the church; therefore, in response to the demand of our times, we are called to be contemplatives, seeking to reawaken a religious sense and awareness. We feel that God is calling us as a community to be a sign of divine presence and activity in the world, a witness to the spiritual dimension of life. Our community is meant to be an invitation to "Come and see"—to see differently, to see the old in a new way, to see a different way of being in God's world. Our service is to pray and to provide space for others to come and pray.

RETREATS

Silent Directed Retreats: Hundreds of people have made directed retreats at Green Bough. Each retreatant meets daily with a spiritual director and is introduced to a method of *praying* Scripture—sitting quietly with a passage, opening one's heart to personal encounter with God. Often a person experiences a felt knowledge of God's presence and personal love, resulting in a sense of belonging and purpose that can be life-changing. There is ample time for praying, journaling, resting, walking, enjoying nature, and participating in the community's daily celebration of Eucharist.

Spiritual Exercises of St. Ignatius: This thirty-day retreat, in which one prays through the life, death and resurrection of Jesus, is a serious commitment of time to heavy-duty prayer. A person longing for a deeper experience of union with God may be drawn to this retreat. It can be helpful in discerning God's will for one's life. Several of our Associates have made the thirty-day retreat. When someone is praying here at that deep concentrated level it is a powerful blessing to our community, and special ties are formed.

Centering Prayer: Almost yearly since 1993 we have offered a nine-month course in Centering Prayer, using video-tapes on the spiritual journey by Father Thomas Keating. The retreat includes instruction in and practice of centering prayer. Participants usually have made a directed retreat and are hungry for some ongoing experience of prayer.

Space for Sojourning: Sojourners stay at Green Bough for an extended time, several weeks to several months, participating in the daily community life of prayer, work and leisure, experiencing the balance of solitude and community provided by Green Bough. A person needing respite from a busy, pressured life may come for the rest and renewal of sabbatical time. Someone in transition, needing time and space for discerning the next leg of the journey, often finds a period of sojourning helpful.

A Particle of Light

Oliver has a particular interest in reaching out to high school and college-age people, perhaps establishing a Sojourner Apprentice term for young adults who are seeking life direction. Aware that touching the earth is a way to reawaken to God's presence in matter, the Sojourner Apprentice would be given hands-in-the-dirt experiences. Practical learning about organic gardening and care for the earth would be undergirded with time to wonder, ponder and cherish the gift of life in the context of contemplative community, finding ways to tie soil and soul together.

Seasonal Observances

New Year's Celebration: On December 31, our evening prayer closes the Octave of Christmas and ushers in the Feast of Mary, Mother of God. New Year's Eve is spent reflecting on the year that is ending and looking toward the year ahead. Poetry, music and silence enrich the celebration. Close to midnight we gather in the Chapel for a time of singing, Scripture reading and intercessions for our world as we welcome the New Year.

We begin New Year's Day with John Wesley's Covenant Service. With the simplicity and challenge of all good liturgy, the service begins with the strong assurance of God's love for us, a love we know from experience; it closes with a prayer in which we abandon ourselves in love to God:

> I am no longer my own but thine. Put me to what thou wilt, rank me with whom thou wilt; put me to doing, put me to suffering; let me be employed for thee or laid aside for thee, exalted for thee or brought low for thee; let me be full, let me be empty; let me have all things, let me have nothing;

I freely and heartily yield all things to thy pleasure and disposal.... Thou art mine, and I am thine. So be it.[1]

Holy Week: Observances begin with Palm Sunday and culminate in the Easter Vigil. On Palm Sunday we read aloud the account of Jesus' entry into Jerusalem, his passion and his death. Entering Holy Week with this story in our hearts and minds sets the stage for the celebration of the Triduum, the three days of Jesus' passion, leading to his death and resurrection.

We begin the Triduum on Holy Thursday with an evening meal around the kitchen table. Then we move to the Chapel for worship that includes foot washing, Eucharist, extinguishing of the light and stripping of the altar. We leave in silence and keep the morning of Good Friday as quiet time to ponder the mystery of Jesus' life.

After lunch we pray the Stations of the Cross, walking slowly around the property, stopping at fourteen stations representing the final hours of the life of Jesus, from his arrest through his being laid in the tomb. At each stop we read Scripture and pray for particular peoples and places of suffering in our world.

As Good Friday draws to a close we return to the Chapel for the Veneration of the Cross. We sit in the darkness and let the events of the day resonate in the silence of our hearts. A line from Good Friday Morning Prayer has set the tone of the day, "The wood of the Cross has brought joy to the world." We return to that line now and ponder the death of Jesus. One by one, people venerate the cross, kneeling before it, placing a hand on it, kissing it. As I sit quietly, I am stirred profoundly by seeing people kneel. The act of kneeling expresses some primordial need to worship, some acknowledgment of right relationship between

Maker and made—the human creature at its most conscious. This simple act of humility opens the fount of wonder and gratitude: My God loves me, even me!

Holy Saturday morning is a time for "waiting by the tomb" with Jesus' friends—the apostles, Mary and the other women. It is a time to feel the grief of loss, the pain of confusion, the fear of chaos, all that is held in the deep sorrow of the heart. The sense of loss awakens the longing for Christ's presence. Without death there is no resurrection.

Around 8:30 in the evening we gather at the Hermitage to kindle the new fire, bless it and light the Christ candle. Steve leads us in procession to the Chapel, stopping three times to sing responsively, "CHRIST OUR LIGHT. THANKS BE TO GOD." As we make our way through the darkness I look up to see the shining stars, knowing that they, too, are singing, "CHRIST OUR LIGHT. THANKS BE TO GOD." They are reminder that we mortals are latecomers to this cosmic act of praise. They seem to say, "Take up your part now. Join in the great chorus begun by the morning stars!" Processing into the dark Chapel we each light a candle from the big Christ candle, the light growing brighter as each person enters. It is Easter, dawning anew. On this night of nights we hear again our faith history as selected Scripture passages are read, beginning with the creation story in Genesis right through the Gospel account of the Resurrection. It is powerful to hear the long story that tells of the movement from darkness into light, slavery into freedom, death into life—this primal journey. God's story. Our story. My story.

Spiritual Direction

Spiritual direction might be defined as *listening with someone for where and how God is at work in his or her life*. This, in large measure, is the service I

Service

offer at Green Bough. Spiritual direction involves deep listening, dipping into the heart of Mystery, open and ready to find one's own story rooted and grounded in the great story of God—a story which is always about Love. Spiritual direction helps us to know the beautiful truth: I am fearfully, wonderfully made—God's beloved.

When I was a young child the words, "Once upon a time…" were like a call to worship. Listening to stories was a part of my early formation, shaping both desire and ability, foretelling my future work as a spiritual director, a listener. If you will tell me your story I will listen, I want to listen. And I have listened, carefully to exquisite stories of people moving through darkness, carrying their light like candles in the wind, shielding their tiny flames, lifting up their stories of sorrow and joy, death and life, longing for wholeness.

When I was eleven years old I saw a spellbinding piece of footage on television showing a young woman in India kissing a cobra. She had been chosen to perform this task so the gods would send rain and a good harvest. Leading a long procession to the mouth of a cave, she carried a basket of the earth's fruits with her. She placed the basket near the cave entrance as an offering; then she stretched her arm into the darkness of the cave and coaxed the cobra out. She swayed hypnotically before the snake, dancing with it, moving back and forth, side to side, slowly drawing closer and closer until she touched its mouth with her lips. I was transfixed, and as a child I was awed by her courage.

Looking back I think of how powerful ritual can be. The girl kissing the cobra—metaphorically what we all have to do in order to receive rain and a good harvest! The breathtaking risk of kissing the cobra—the willingness to lean into the darkness of oneself and embrace what one finds there, all for the sake of wholeness. The shadow embraced yields the golden gift. To go to the cave, the place we would prefer not to go; to call out the cobra, to face the pain or loss or fear we would rather not face—this is the hard labor of creativity. To kiss death is to receive life. I think this ritual was powerful to me as a child because it gave me a glimpse of what I knew intuitively but could not have expressed at that early age. It awakened me to something I could begin to grapple with until it could break more clearly into my consciousness many years later. It held the truth of wholeness, fullness and fruition before me until I was mature enough to receive it. Jesus and Judas kissed one another. I once heard an old Jesuit say that the prayer of Jesus, the Divine Healer, brought Judas to him. I hold the mystery of that in my heart.

God does not waste anything. Everything in a person's life is valuable. Pain must not be wasted—it is a teacher to be honored. One of my mentors said, "If you are going to do any spiritual work you will have to live without eyelids. You won't be allowed to blink. You must look at everything." The spiritual life is not about escaping; it is about embracing. In spiritual direction we open to the presence of Christ—to the courage and deep peace of the One who held heaven and earth together on a cross.

When the teller and the listener sit together, attentive to the presence of the Holy Spirit, surprising things happen. In that awesome moment the process of healing can begin, turning bane into blessing. The important thing is that one's story be told and heard, and that it be welcomed by both oneself and another. When accepted and loved, pain is denied the authority to destroy life. Instead, it moves us toward wholeness in which the darkness itself becomes radiant and all of life can be lived.

Service

In spiritual direction there are times to be fierce and times to be gentle. Both qualities are necessary—and one has to be careful with both. The spiritual director's work is to listen with the other until God's voice is recognized among all the other competing voices. The desire of the director is to help and heal, or more precisely, to offer oneself to God to be used in the divine work of healing. This may require fierce objectivity as well as gentle sympathy. God takes the wounds of the director and turns them into compassion.

I love Scripture, and I almost always use it in spiritual direction. My Jesuit training, as well as my Methodist upbringing, confirms the gift of it. Scripture sets me in a context that spans ages and worlds, giving me something bigger and older and deeper than my personal ideas and opinions to lean on. It is a great source of wisdom that informs, challenges and strengthens. Scripture is alive and cuts like a two-edged sword slicing deep, opening up thoughts and motives, laying bare all that is hidden, so that healing can come.[2] Grace reveals the truth about oneself: God has "searched me and known me." I am utterly known and utterly loved. That is the firm foundation on which faith rests, the fertile ground for life abundant.

In a long ago dream I was given important insight into the way my life would unfold. In the dream I was sitting on the steps of First United Methodist Church in Swainsboro, Georgia, the church in which I was raised, the church I loved. Suddenly there were seashells all over the steps, a vast array glistening and beautiful. As I reflected on the dream it seemed that the seashells, symbol of baptism, were my spiritual children. I, who had longed for children would, through my work as a spiritual director, both give birth to life and be its mid-wife too.

I felt that the steps on which I sat pointed to my place in the church. I was coming to realize that I would never have a central place in the church. I would live out my faith on the steps, on the border between the church and the world. I was not even on the porch. The steps marked that liminal space of entry and departure for people. With dawning clarity it seemed to me that my vocation lay in that place of threshold, giving solace and support to those who were coming into and those who were leaving church. The Psalmist assures us that, "God guards our going out and our coming in."[3]

Most of the people who come to Green Bough are struggling in some way with the church. My own faith history has made me a magnet for these particular people. My calling as spiritual director is at God's service. For this I seem to have been created. I have been placed at Green Bough as a sentinel of the border to guard and guide, comfort and encourage. God's doing.

I hold with Irenaeus, who long ago said, "The glory of God is a human being fully alive." The glory of God is shining in every person—each one *a particle of light*. I see it up close in those who come for direction. People come with genuine desire for the "something more" that leads to fullness of life. I believe the universal human longing is to experience the Divine Center where the radiance of God's love transforms everything. And when we enter that place of awe we say—if we can say anything at all—"O the depth of the riches and wisdom and knowledge of God!"[4]

I speak to people of God's love, assuring them that God has drawn them to this moment and this place. My message is always the same: We belong to God and there is nowhere we can be that is outside of God. Whether coming in or going out, we belong to God. God's desire for each of us is that we be awake, vibrant human beings. We are free to live fully, intensely, aware and grateful in every place, moment and circumstance—because nothing is outside of God. All of life can be lived. It is all gift. Particles of light are created to shine!

Finally, spiritual direction—this sitting as companion to another in the presence of the Spirit—is a Communion. Years ago, near the end of my 30-day Ignatian retreat, I was praying the Gospel accounts of the death of Jesus. I was instructed to enter into the story in such a way that it would enter into me and become my story. I was to "wait by the tomb" with the women and the disciples, watching with them, feeling the sorrow, confusion and loss they would have experienced at Jesus' death. For my prayer time I went to a secluded spot surrounded by shrubbery and sat down on a bench, letting myself feel the loneliness and emptiness that come after the death of a loved one. I had been sitting for a long time, feeling a rising longing for Jesus' presence, when out of the surrounding bushes crawled a little African-American boy, with an orange soda and a paper bag. He came and sat down beside me. An unexpected wave of joy swept over me. He edged closer to me, and we sat quietly for a while, both of us, I believe, somehow comforted by one another's presence. Then he opened the bag he was holding and said, "You want some cookies?" With that question my eyes were opened. Christ had come to me! Here I was being offered *companionship*. Companions, after all, are the *ones with whom we share bread*. (From the Latin *com* means 'with,' *panis* means 'bread,' making our companions 'those with whom we break bread'.) Christ was right here, present, offering the gift of Himself to me. Here was Jesus sitting beside me with soda and cookies, come to feed me. This was Communion. Spiritual direction is something like that.

Vision, prayer, community, service—these are the contours that hold this community, giving it shape and purpose. Green Bough itself is a place of succor, a place of milk and honey, bread and wine; a place of welcome. We have seen here, with our own eyes, something of the power of presence. When we gather at the Table we remember the gift of Christ's life lived *for* us, given *for* us. "Take; eat; this is my body given for you." Christ also gives himself *to* us. As we swallow the gifts placed in our hands we respond in our hearts: *Let us receive you; let us be you.* It is Christ we receive and Christ we become. It is Christ who speaks through us: "Take, eat. This is my body given for you." It is Christ speaking to Christ. For in truth, it is Christ who comes hungry asking: "Have you something here to eat?" And it is Christ who feeds: "Take; eat...." It is Christ himself who is bread, wine, guest, host and table. Christ, all in all.

In his book, *Clowning in Rome*, Henri Nouwen says, "To contemplate is to *see*, and to minister is to *make visible*; the contemplative life is a life of vision and the life of ministry is a life in which this vision is revealed to others."[5] These words seem to compass both aspects of our calling: first, to be a presence of prayer and second, to provide a place for others to come and pray.

The community of Green Bough is a place where contemplation and service meet—for the sake of revealing the vision. *It is my prayer that Green Bough, in both its placed and scattered aspects, will make visible what it has seen: God's love.* God's love present with us, in us, through us. One small community can do that. One person can do that. We are here to give witness to a vision of life together, where peace, justice, joy and compassion hold sway.

Service

As we kindle the new light at the Easter Vigil we pray that "our hearts and minds may also be kindled with holy desire to shine forth with the brightness of Christ's rising…." We pray, and God does the unimaginable. We who are not very bright, who are dull and dim about almost everything—WE are *kindled and sent* to give luster to the night until it is as bright as the day. Stumbling, limping and laughing at the ludicrousness of it, we go into the darkness with holy desire to shine forth: to be Christ-light in the world. We must *see* who we are. We must *be* who we are in the presence of God and one another.

Every person carries a particle of light—God hidden in us, tucked into our unsuspecting hearts. Given this light, we are obliged to bear witness. As Gabriel Marcel said, "to keep it to myself would be equivalent to extinguishing it." We do not own this gift. We are stewards of it. Whoever we are, wherever we are, we are asked to tend it and let it shine for God's glory and the common good of God's world. What we carry—this unique, creative gift—is to be offered back to God for the ongoing, unfolding adventure of life.

Chapter 16

AMEN

Before leaving the Chapel after Evening Prayer I stopped once more in front of the hovering dove holding the green bough in its beak. The beautiful stained glass was illumined by soft afternoon light. The window came from the old Methodist Church in Swainsboro, the building in which I worshipped as a child. When the church moved to a new site in 1957 the building was sold, and the lovely old windows were left behind. They recently came up for sale, and a friend purchased this particular one for Green Bough. Standing before the window, I reached out to touch the bough, and I felt the bird with its radiant wings, the dear Spirit itself, settle peacefully into my heart. Wonder, the gift of childhood, and surrender, the gift of old age, are the joyous notes that rise in me.

This long work of writing is drawing to an end. Many stories are left untold, and I am tempted to tell just one more, but I will not. I have treasured this time of remembering, reflecting and relating. I have experienced it as prayer. Now the time has come to say, AMEN. So be it!

Amen

Life is good! Good indeed! From the vantage point of 76 years I can say in all honesty, "I could not have asked for more!" Thirty of my years have come and gone here at Green Bough.

The goodness was embodied in Green Bough's 30th anniversary as we raised the white tent of celebration with its graceful, curved top. The tent defined the space well and cast a radiant glow over things underneath it. We seemed to be sitting under the wings of the Dove, sheltered and held close together. Family, friends and Associates were gathered with us to celebrate. We prayed Morning Prayer, listened to the music of the folk duo Liz and Tim, sang hymns, danced and shared memories of Green Bough. My heart stirred as people spoke, often beginning "I don't have words to express…." Then with tenderness and gratitude, they told of the love, healing and hope they found in the quiet of this place, in the beauty of its setting among fields and trees, in the gift of community and belonging. They spoke of awakening anew to God and the "something more" of life. Their beautiful faces and heartfelt devotion were shining with light. The radiance under the tent allowed us to look beyond the seen and catch a glimpse of the Unseen. I felt myself in that in-between place where visible and invisible worlds meet, where the seen is animated by the Unseen. I felt as if I were looking through the thin veil and into another world, where the sweet presences of those gone before us hovered near. So many precious faces, seen and unseen. The sheer gift of all that love! All day the wind swept through the space, giving evidence of the Spirit's presence blessing us beyond all telling.

And then across the space I saw Steve, my comrade of all these thirty years, and my heart melted; and Oliver, who has been with us for five years, and already so very dear. I am blessed beyond measure to share with these men this calling to life at Green Bough. "I don't have words to express" what I feel for them, but love, gratitude, respect, and awe would top the list. With affection I often call them "my dear'sts." They show me the face of Christ each day.

Now I have sat and watched the tent-takers come and take down the lovely canopy that shaded us and held us as we celebrated. They have folded it up and taken it away. It was the 'tent of meeting' and the 'big top' all rolled into one. Thirty years is well worth celebrating. "It is right, and a good and joyful thing, to give thanks," we pray at Eucharist. Our hearts were made full by the beautiful day of remembrance and thanksgiving. And now we open our arms to this day, and to all our tomorrows, "persuaded that God is able to keep that which we've committed to Him until that day."[1]

Postlude

A Particle of Light

Magdalene Day Talk, July 19, 2008

The Magdalene Project, "founded in 2000 by six Atlanta women to promote the lives of holy women of the past as models of spiritual transformation for women and men of today," sponsored ten annual Magdalene Celebrations. Committee members Lalor Cadley, chairperson, and Barb Meinert are Green Bough Associates and were responsible for honoring me. Each year they presented the "Judy Schubert Magdalene Award for a woman of courage and vision exhibiting the qualities of Mary of Magdala." In 2008 I was recipient of that award. This is the talk I gave at the celebration in Atlanta.

Thank you. This is an honor. Thank you to the Magdalene Day Committee. You have planned and prepared a wonderful gathering for us today. A special thanks to Steve who bears the Christ-light for me each day and has been my comrade for many years now. Thank you for who you are and for life shared. I feel the presence of precious ones gone before me, and give thanks for them. I am certain you have made my mama and daddy smile. And a salute to Judy Schubert, who meant so much to so many of you and in whose memory this award is given. I am surrounded here by many people I know, people whom I love and who love me. What a treasure of a time. Being together is the sweetest gift. Thank you!

I know I am here because I have given birth to a beautiful daughter named Green Bough, that little House of Prayer, which my friend Hannah, Sr. Peter Claver, referred to as an "island of sanity in an insane world." My daughter has reached her majority. It was 21 years ago that Steve and I moved to Scott. We brought with us a burning longing to

POSTLUDE

love with abandon the God who first loved us. We came with the understanding that our calling was first of all to pray and to be a presence of prayer, whether anyone else ever came or not. The second part of the calling was to provide sacred space for others to come and pray, if that was what God wanted. And people have come. A wonderful stream of magnificence.

We live as a Christian community with a rule of life and a daily round of prayer. There is no over-estimating the value of habits that support and encourage us in the life of faith. Habits, not to make God love us more—as if God needs to grow in love. These habits are to help *us* grow in love of God and neighbor. The practice of devotion is the wisdom of the ages. We keep the lamp alight for weary pilgrims. We create a little space of peace and balance in a world of frantic activity—a place of prayer to remind us that we belong to God, that God's life and love flow through us, and that we are privileged to serve God's world in its need.

This time last week I was making blueberry jam. I had just talked with Lalor on the phone. She had called to give me some instructions for Magdalene Day. As we talked, I found myself jumping ahead a week, getting really anxious, saying to myself, "What am I going to say to those women next week?" A voice deep inside me said, "Say to them what I say to you. 'You are making blueberry jam. Be present and attentive to this task. *This* moment is the field where the treasure lies. This is the day I give you.'" So, I returned to the present moment and did what I was doing and thoroughly enjoyed it. I say to us here: "God has made this day and given it to us. Let us take joy in it."

We see people every day who are living somewhere else, in the future or in the past. Some have signs hanging on their noses: Sorry, not home.

Out to lunch. Vegetable inside. The simple antidote to absentee living is prayer, quiet, stillness…daily. We long to live a life of presence. Living somewhere else all the time wears us out. We were made for the present, and 'not being at home' disconnects us from our center, from the source of our energy. The deep-dwelling Christ in us is longing to draw us out of the shallows and down into the Divine Heart. Calling us to come home, to be present in the moment because that is where we encounter God.

What Green Bough provides is a prayer-soaked place for slowing down, being still, listening attentively to Scripture, to nature, to one's heart, to one's life, eating a good meal, hearing a poem, participating in Eucharist, being present through the moments of the day. So simple, really: place and time to re-awaken to the Source of life whose current runs through all our days, making the ordinary extraordinary, turning the water into wine.

March 30th was my 66th birthday, and my intention had been to sleep in on that morning. Steve and I were journeying, on the way to a 5-day retreat in Louisiana, and we had stopped along the way to spend the night. Feeling tired and weary I went to bed, expecting to rise leisurely the next morning. Well, at 6:00 a.m. the trumpet of Gabriel sounded—Awake! Arise! The loudest alarm clock I've ever heard had gone off right next to my bed. I sat straight up, got the thing turned off, and lay back down, only to have it sound again after 10 minutes. It was not lost on me, this wake-up call on the morning of my birthday. It was Gabriel, with trumpet in hand, for sure. But I think the trumpet was for emphasis, not final call. This was annunciation, re-annunciation, the ongoing life with God. My name was spoken again. My calling was announced again. And that old desire in me was fresh and strong. Yes. I belong to You. Do

POSTLUDE

with me what you will. Wake me up. Help me to live with more and more awareness and presence.

Prayer awakens us. The spiritual journey is an ongoing awakening. Awakening to the *wonder of having been given the gift of life.* Awakening to the *wonder of God's presence with us and in us, and that it is our birthright to live in that presence.* Awakening to the *wonder that God needs us as co-creators, needs us to help complete creation.* Along the journey I have learned that most often the first response to God's overture is, "Oh." "Oh?" "Oohh." "Oooooh." It's a response that lends itself to many variations. After we've gotten over the Oh, we come to the depth response of gratitude. Thank you.

I want to share three pictures from the album of my life. In each you will see those two old friends, prayer and awakening, holding hands. And the caption under each is Thank You.

1st Picture: Years ago at Jekyll Island on a Sunday evening I sat alone on the beach, beside that mighty, mysterious old womb of life—the Fertile Feminine. With the roar of the ocean as background music, I was praying the Sunday Evening Office. A line from Psalm 110 enthralled me: "From the womb before the dawn I begot you."[1] "From the *womb* before the dawn I begot you." "From the womb *before the dawn* I begot you." "From the womb before the dawn *I* begot *you*." I stopped right there and said, "Oh...." God has been laboring from the beginning to bring each of us forth, and I understood that that evening. I understood it personally. God continues to labor in us and for us, so that we can come into the fullness of who we are meant to be. God needs us and wants us to join in that Divine laboring on behalf of and for the sake of the world God so loves, that ALL might come into fullness. My journey curved toward Green Bough that night.

2nd Picture: I wish I could connect every child with a wise old woman, an old grandmother. When I was a little girl my grandmother Key stayed with us a lot after my granddaddy died. She slept in the bed with me. After we had knelt and prayed, we climbed into bed, and there in the quiet, dark bedroom she would talk to me. She would tell me how her heart ached for poor people and how she felt such tenderness toward the plight of black people—colored was the word we used in those days. She would describe how hard life was for most people. As she talked softly in the night, I could feel my own heart open, and when she fell asleep the darkness would become deep and holy as the silence wrapped around me, and I felt the suffering of the world, the hurt of people near and far—though they all seemed near in that moment, all right inside my heart. I somehow knew that God felt all that tenderness, and that God was tying my heart to the needs of the world. I think how formative those nighttime conversations were, a little opening up of my world, followed by the quiet, and held there in the dark, with time to ponder and let it all sink in. I was learning Lectio Divina. Ooohhh.

3rd Picture: A couple of weeks ago I got up early one morning, washed my face and went to sit on the porch. It was quiet and still outside, a heavy mist hung over the field. The rain from the night had wet down the earth, and the trees stood tall, each leaf dripping water as if each one had just washed its little face. As I sat there our cat Penelope ambled over and sat beside me. She washed her face, dampening her paws and rubbing her mouth, eyes, nose and ears. After a while I became aware of a rabbit in the distance, sitting at full alert. As I watched, the bunny began washing its face, licking its paws and dabbing at its face. I felt the delight of knowing myself as a creature among creatures with more similarities than I'd probably care to own. There we all were, faces washed. As I soaked long in that bath of quiet a line from Emerson's

Postlude

journal floated up into my mind: "Jones Very said he felt it an honor to wash his face, being, as it was, the temple of the Spirit." I laughed out loud. Oooohhhh.

God indwells us all. And so we are honored. How our souls hunger and thirst for that awareness. We forget. That morning re-awakened in me the memory of God's presence in all things. A deep knowing already in us, somehow forgotten in the hurry of life. I re-membered all creation as I sat in the stillness of that morning. And God re-membered me in the moment of awakening, drawing me deep into the Divine Heart where I could know once again that I am one with God, and one with all God's creation.

How do we keep remembering who we are, whose we are? How do we live out of and into the Fertile Feminine? Prayer, of course. Stillness and quiet—daily! "Oh." We celebrate Mary today. She is the best of guides in this, and so we say: Mary, Temple of the Spirit, teach us to treasure and to ponder. Teach us to pray, so that our hearts might be able to carry the seed of Love, to give birth to Love in a thousand small ways day by day, to swaddle Love and tend it at midnight, and help it grow in every way we can.

Steve and I invite you to come to Green Bough.

A Particle of Light

25th Anniversary, September 8, 2012

A talk given to Green Bough Associates at our 25th Anniversary celebration.

Twenty-five years! So long and so short. How can it be? I give thanks for this place, this life, my most treasured comrade of the journey, Steve. I give thanks for you, my precious community visible.

"Come let us praise the Lord; in God is all our delight." This was the opening antiphon of Morning Prayer today, and it holds for me the essence of Green Bough. "Come let us praise the Lord; in God is all our delight." To ground me, I touched the ring I have worn for many years. Steve wears one too. It bears the inscription: THOU ALONE.

I was sitting on the side porch of the Anchorhold—one of my favorite places on all the earth—and I saw anew the beauty of this very ordinary place—the green pines against the blue sky, the long view across the field to the wood's edge, the red roses in bloom along the edge of the bell tower garden, the trees we planted as tiny twigs now grown immense. I could see Christ's smile coming to us through the beauty of nature. I could hear again Christ saying, "Be a presence of prayer in this place, and make for me a space for people to come and join you in prayer." My heart brimmed with thanks that I could be a part of all this, because I know it has come into being at Christ's bidding.

As I continued to sit, an antiphon that we sometimes sing slipped into my mind: "My heart thirsts for you Lord, like the desert thirsts for rain. It is your face I long for. You alone are life to me." With my eyes I drank and drank. I long to see Your face wherever I look, to see You in all your creation.

Postlude

And now I look out over this gathering. Such beauty! Every face showing me the face of Christ. I want to bow before you. How can I say thank you? Each of you more beautiful than you know. Each of you unique, your name called in the beginning. Our Mother Christ laboring from the beginning, to bring you forth that you might be God's glory in this time, in this place. The precious gift of life—given to be given.

I have always loved candles. And this year has been a year of candles for me. For my birthday Lea brought 70 candles, arranged them beautifully on an orange cloth on the floor in front of the altar. They were all alight when I walked into the chapel that night in March. It was a breathtaking sight, and I was totally surprised. When everyone was in place for Night Prayer, I was asked to light the large candle in the center. After I lit it and sat down, it suddenly flared, spewing sparks of light all around, making us gasp. Then, I was aware last evening in the chapel when Steve, Linda and I were praying Evening Prayer, how inviting the soft glow of the candles was. Every night when we light them I can feel myself being drawn deep into the heart of God—and wanting to go there.

Years ago, just before I came here, I was attending Catholic Mass at the Jesuit Center in Pennsylvania. It was late afternoon, and the sun coming through the chapel windows touched the clear glass cup of wine on the altar in such a way that it seemed to me like a chalice full of fire. As I watched people drinking from the cup I thought, "We swallow the fire of God and dreams are set aflame." This room tonight is full of the dreams of God, each of us carrying in ourselves the particular dream set aflame in us—dreams of *peace* in a world of war and conflict; dreams of *light* in a world of darkness; dreams of *healing and wholeness* in a wounded and broken world; dreams of *truth* in a world of lies; dreams of *justice* in a world of injustice, dreams that have risen out of prayer, the faithful prayer of longing hearts, prayer that reminds us that we are rooted and grounded in the very heart of Love. Prayer that is our breath as we live our lives in the various places God has put us. Prayer that enables us to carry the world, to hold it and rock it in its need, just the way Mary rocked her Baby—as an old spiritual says, "Every time that little Baby cried she rocked it in a weary land." Prayer that opens our hearts to listen so that in the midnight hour when we are awake and cannot sleep, we can hear the call to join all intercessors in holding the wounds of the earth in God's love. Prayer that opens our eyes so that we can see the face of Christ wherever we look. We, of this community of Green Bough, are called to prayer. It keeps kindled the fire of our dreams.

And so, my dear hearts, on this 25th anniversary of Green Bough, I say to you: *pray, pray always*.

Nearly every night as Steve and I leave the Old House to go to our own little abodes, we look up at the beautiful night sky and feel the presence of Mystery. For several months in the spring, each night we would look up and see two stars through a clearing circled by tree branches. They were like two bright eyes looking down at us. I would say to Steve, "We are being watched," and I'd wave at them. Steve would wink his flashlight at them. I was always reminded of Teresa of Avila's description of her prayer: "When I pray I am looking at the One who is looking at me." May we know we are watched by the tenderest eyes. May we look back with love. May we know we are prayed even as we pray.

Postlude

Getting the Break I Needed

On September 12, 2013, midway my 71st year, I broke my leg and found myself almost totally dependent on the help of others. I can't say that I recommend the experience, but I can say that I would not have missed it for the world. It was a time full of love and life lessons. I can name the six months of being hobbled as a time when the dawn from on high broke upon me, dazzling my darkness. I felt intimately the entwining of light and dark. One of the great lessons of the experience was the faithfulness of light in the darkness. Perhaps I have always known this at some level. Perhaps it is why my heart leaps at the sight of a starry night sky.

I was enclosed in the Anchorhold for three months, unable to get myself in and out of the space. The day I came home from the hospital, from my wheel chair I took a questioning look at my predicament, and something in me said firmly, "Do not fear. Give yourself to this experience." During the weeks of enclosure my heart opened to receive with love and joy the long days in the Anchorhold. Many people expressed concern about my being confined and unable to go and come at will. One day near the end of the three months of confinement, at the close of a session of spiritual direction, the woman I had been sitting with looked at this anchoress and said with amazing understanding, "You will have a hard time leaving this space, won't you?" She was right. And yet I was ready. It was time. I gradually entered into a more active life again, moving from a walker to a cane, and then stepping, with growing confidence, into the old patterns and routines of life at Green Bough. After my birthday, I knew I wanted to speak from my heart about the experience. And so in early April, soon after turning 72, I wrote a letter.

A Particle of Light

Early April, 2014

Dear Ones,

Bane and blessing often walk hand in hand. So it is true for me to say that I finally got the break I needed. Truth is, it was a small difficulty in the overall scheme of things—but a big one for me. There seemed to be no reason for the fall. People ask, but I can't explain it. The moment was shadowed. The sole of my right shoe gripped the floor—it stayed in place and I fell over. As I fell I heard the bone snap, and though it happened fast it also happened in slow motion. I who had never broken a bone, never been hospitalized, and not been to a doctor in 30 years—I was down. And oddly, even as I was falling the thought flashed clearly into my mind: *give yourself fully to this experience, to whatever it holds.* I so often say to people, "Learn from your experience. Don't waste it. Let your pain expand you. Look for God in it." And I knew without a doubt that was what I was to do with this. I knew I was not to resist anything. I was to be as open as possible to whatever lay ahead. I was to receive the experience as gift, and give myself to it. That immediate clarity itself was gift.

"Dependent on the kindness of strangers." I skimmed over these words recently, almost missing them. But something drew me back to them. I repeated them several times, sensing a sweetness there and wondering why. Slowly it occurred to me that they described those first hours after my accident. There were ambulance drivers, hospital staff, technicians, nurses and doctors who gave the kindest care. Not one of them did I know. Not one of them did I choose. They just showed up, strangers who were kind. And I depended on their kindness. When the surgeon arrived it never crossed my mind to ask anything about him. He came

Postlude

into the room, and he became *my* surgeon. I trusted he had been sent to me.

Dr. Fried (or Dr. Friend as I sometimes think of him). As I reflect on that mid-September surgery in the early morning of Friday the 13th, I imagine him standing, like Ezekiel in the valley full of bones. In the service of healing, his hands prophesied, resetting my leg, putting bone, sinew and flesh back together, so that new life might be breathed into dry bones. I am amazed at what can be done medically and amazed at the miracle of healing. I am aware that not too many years ago a break like I suffered would have left a person crippled for life. And not too long ago any surgery or setting of bones would have been done without anesthesia or pain medication. I am thankful that I live in a time and place to benefit from the wonders of modern medicine. Dr. Fried, for all I know of that surgery, may have used scotch tape, safety pins, gem clips and rubber bands, but all the x-ray shows is a steel plate with screws that looks a lot like a toothbrush inserted in my ankle. And now I walk again and am deeply grateful. Healing did not happen overnight. It was a slow and gradual process. Six months passed before he released me from his care. His office staff congratulated me on my graduation.

Through this long time Steve and Oliver were present day and night. What can I say about such gifts? They are strongholds for me—and shining stars. They moved swiftly into "keep calm and carry on" mode—taking care of Green Bough, taking care of my needs, giving me a deepened appreciation of the gift of community. We kept our schedule of common prayer throughout these month. And thanks to them, we continued to provide retreat, quiet space, fine meals, and worship for people who came. I kept my schedule of spiritual direction the entire time. My confinement made life harder for everyone. I had become a 'high maintenance woman'—but I never felt resentment or annoyance from anyone, only kindness and loving care. Patience, laughter and tears—ingredients of love. We learned a lot about ourselves and about our community as we gave ourselves to the work of "making the bitter valley a place of springs."[2]

When I returned home from the hospital Steve and Oliver, one on either side of me, carried me up the steps and into the Anchorhold, and there I stayed except for occasional times when Oliver took me to see the doctor. I can say from my heart that the time of enclosure was good, very good. Right away two things happened that set me up for the long weeks ahead.

On my second day home I got into the wheel chair Steve had found for me to use and maneuvered it awkwardly into the sitting room. As I sat in the early morning darkness, longing to be still and quiet, but feeling a little frustrated and anxious, a memory surfaced. It must have been around 1972-74 that the event occurred, but it seemed as if it were yesterday. I was at a dance. A couple was dancing, and the man was in a wheel chair. He was dancing his heart out—spinning, dipping, bowing, circling the woman, moving away from her, moving toward her. It was glorious to see. The rest of us slowly stopped dancing and just stood and watched. Joy, energy, abandon, gratitude were radiating out from him. I could feel it. And as I stood there I remember saying, "God, whatever my circumstances in life, help me to dance like the man in the wheel chair. That's how I want to live." As I let the memory fill me I felt the courage come. I can do this! I can be a woman with a broken leg, and I can love life—just as it is. I can give myself fully to this situation and fully receive the gift of this time.

Postlude

Then the next morning I woke up with a powerful dream clearly in my consciousness: I was in a place of chaos, a microcosm of the world, being shown venues of suffering and struggle. Moving from place to place, I knew I was to look with open eyes at the strife and confusion, to really see the pain everywhere, to know it and feel it. Then I saw a larger than life figure dressed in white priestly robes, shining, a numinous figure. He moved peacefully into the midst of the chaos, blessing it all. I spoke to him and he called me by name. I told him I had lost my purse, my cell phone and my keys. They may have been stolen. At any rate I had lost control. I asked him to call Steve to come for me. He said that I could drive his car home and that Steve would help me return it in the morning. He then handed me a splendid, oversized ring of old ornate keys with a round golden head of Pope Francis on it. I felt they were spiritual keys, for opening inner rooms and ancient spaces. My ankle was hurting. I was tired and looking for the car. The drama was not over. Then I became aware of a beautiful, spacious monastery right before me.

I awoke with a deep assurance that in the midst of this chaotic, difficult period of my life in which I had so little control, the blessing of Christ's presence would cover me and help me through—blessing it all. I had lost my purse, my cell phone, my keys. Indeed I had lost my independence, my self as I had known it. In the Anchorhold I had poor to no telephone reception and communication was limited. Unable to drive, I had no use for car keys. Those were gone, at least for the time being. This was a time for discovering deeper self, deeper communion, deeper journeying. What I was given was Christ's presence in the midst of my chaos, covering it all with peace; Christ moving over the troubled places with blessing. A friend pointed out to me that the keys given me were not only about opening inner spiritual places but also were about my own inner power and authority being given to me to take up in a new and more intentional way. I don't fully understand what that means, but I trust it will become clear.

I felt the dream was speaking not only about my personal life but also about our planet, about the world. There is a beautiful, spacious monastery that sits at the heart of it all, if only we can see. We don't have to look somewhere else or live in some other time or place. Light shines in the darkness. In the midst of chaos and confusion there is peace beyond our understanding. In the midst of our pain is our healing. In our letting go we receive gift beyond measure. Life abides steady in the realm of all our dyings. A hard, sweet knowing.

Another insight was given me a few weeks after my fall. I have long thought a part of my vocation was to be an anchoress, even my little house is called the Anchorhold. In medieval times there were women called to live as solitaries who would hold in prayer the needs of both the church and the world. When they felt their calling was solid they would have themselves sealed into a room built onto the side of a church, becoming dependent on the community for food and drink. There were two windows in the room, one which looked into the church and one out onto the world. The anchoress thus was available to participate in the worship of the church and was available to the world for anyone who wanted to come for counsel or comfort or to bring food. Julian of Norwich the most famous medieval anchoress lived in the 1300-1400's. But this strange vocation has lasted through the centuries. When I worked at the women's shelter in Rome, Georgia someone brought me a book called *Wide Neighborhoods*. It was the autobiography of Mary Breckinridge, who founded the Frontier Nursing Service in Appalachia in 1925. She had been greatly influenced by an anchoress named Adeline

Postlude

she had met in England. As I read that book in the early 1980's, I was fascinated by her description of a modern-day anchoress and found the calling compelling. And so for years I have thought of myself as, in part, an anchoress—broadly interpreted, of course. This time of enclosure was my *sealing in*. And though for me it would not be permanent, the weeks inside my anchorhold gave me some experience of being closeted for a purpose: to pray for *all* who love and serve God and to pray for our fractured and fractious world that God so loves.

I was truly blessed in and by this time of enclosure. I was dependent, to be sure, and my community brought me food in abundance, flowers, books and even a gel cushion to ease my sitting. Connie was my angel who showed up daily to help with housecleaning, laundry and many other tasks I could not do. There were the loveliest visits from my family and friends; phone calls when the anchorhold could get decent reception; cards, notes, and chocolates, plus movies for entertainment. Then there were retreatants at Green Bough most of this time, who came for spiritual direction. The window onto the world functioned well. And so did the window into the church. Steve, Oliver and I prayed Morning Prayer daily, and I was brought bread and wine after every Eucharist. I inhaled, absorbed, swam in and swallowed this time. It was profound and delightful to be still, to pray, to read, to sit quietly, to feel deeply, to "taste and see the goodness of God."[3] It was pure gift.

As I healed and grew stronger I began to feel my energy moving outward again. And yet I *knew* I must stay still. A resonant chord sounded in me. This was the secret of grace. This was the truth being told me: all is gift. I was being reminded not to hurry through the end of this time of enclosure. I needed most of all to practice the Sacrament of the Present moment, the leading practice of our Green Bough Rule. I needed simply to be present, to give myself to now, to see the moment as chalice and paten in which God gives Himself fully to me, to us all. All I can say is, "Thanks, thanks for everything!"

On the 30th of March I turned 72. I am out of my time of enclosure, moving freely again in the world. I am well in the deeps of my being.

For my birthday Steve and I went to Atlanta for a gathering of area Green Bough Associates. We saw the IMAX movie, *Jerusalem*. It featured three lovely young women, one Jewish, one Christian, one Muslim. They spoke of their faiths, their practices, their concerns, their hopes and longings for peace. They each took us on a tour of their part of the golden city, so beautiful, so ancient, so divided and troubled. The city we call holy. Everywhere was teeming with the energy of life. At the end all three of the young women were shown on screen looking off in different directions, while the narrator voiced the hope that one day we would learn to truly see one another. That is my hope too, that we learn to see through the borders and barriers that keep us blinded to each other.

I believe my task in the remaining years of my life is *to live with eyes wide open and to transform this time and place which I have been given— and to be transformed by it.*

The Psalmist's words become mine:

> For love of my family and friends I say: "Peace upon you!"
> For love of the house of God I will ask for your good.[4]

Green Bough Rule of Life

Accept all as coming from God,
Do all for God,
Offer all to God,

And seek ardently
the perfection of Charity
and the love of the Cross.

Raissa Maritain
Rule of Life

"You shall love the Lord your God
with all your heart,
with all your soul,
with all your mind
and with all your strength." (*Mk. 12:30*)

Acknowledging God as Giver of life
and creator of all that is,
we seek to love God wholly.

In response to the Divine Initiative
we yield ourselves in love to Love.

"And you shall love your neighbor as yourself."
(*Mk. 12:31*)

Acknowledging all persons as created by God
and loved by God,
we seek to respond to others in love,
serving each as Christ commands.

This rule, joyfully chosen,
is to enable us to love God more fully
and to live rightly as a part of God's creation.
It is a discipline to help us grow day by day
in the life of Christ.

Our calling to a life of prayer
is a service in the world, bearing witness
to God's longing for all people
to be in union with Divine Love.
"May they all be one:
as you, Father, are in me, and I in you,
so also may they be in us,
that the world may believe that you sent me."
(Jn. 17:21)

I
Sacrament of the Present Moment

In gratitude for the gift of life
we will seek to be aware of God
present in every moment,
trusting that as we respond in faith
to the duties of each day
God is revealed.

The Word made flesh and dwelling among us
shows his glory
in the ordinary circumstances of daily life,
in the neighbor's need,
in the beauty of creation,
in the tasks set before us,
and in the rub of community life.

In these moments we would see
and hear
and taste
and touch
the goodness of God.
And we would ask the Holy Spirit
to guide our thoughts
and words
and actions
that we might glorify God in all.

II
Prayer

In recognition of God's longing for us
and our longing for God
we will set aside a time each day
for both common prayer
and personal prayer.

As a part of the whole people of God,
we pray the prayer of the Church,
the Office of the Psalms.
This corporate prayer,
based on the liturgical year,
is the primary expression
of our life together in Christ.
As we pray the Office
we experience the mystery
of Jesus' presence in us.

Remembering God's command and promise
we will delight in the Lord
by keeping the Sabbath holy.

As individual members of the Body of Christ,
we will give ourselves to personal prayer,
to being with God
and to listening for His word to us.

These times set aside for prayer,
corporate and personal,
are to enable us to pray at all times,
to live prayerfully.

III
Simplicity

Acknowledging God as Giver and Sustainer of life
we will order our lives in simplicity,
relying on God's Providence.
We will seek daily to unclutter our lives
by letting go of things, concerns and habits
that divide our hearts
and keep us from Simplicity itself.

We will content ourselves
with the place and provision God grants
and call to mind each day
the plight of the poor
and the needs of the world's peoples.

We will order our day
 so that we will have time—
time for God,
time for people,
time for ourselves,
observing a rhythm of work and leisure.

Ordinarily the morning
will be given to reflective activities,
to prayer, reading and correspondence;
the afternoon to physical labor;
the evening to community life and nurture
through the company of the faithful.

IV
Silence and Solitude

In response to God's one true Word,
the Word our hearts long for,
we will spend time daily
in silence and in solitude.

In silence and solitude
we listen for the Word, Christ,
present in the beginning and dwelling within us.

We are drawn beyond division,
into the mystery of unity in Christ,
in whom all things in the heavens and on earth
are made one.

The Word is spoken to us personally,
and in the solitude of the heart,
our true identity is revealed.

Time set aside for silence and solitude
creates an awareness of God's Word
and cultivates an attitude

of attentiveness and receptivity,
enabling us to think
and speak
and act
in response to God's word throughout the day.

V
Spiritual Direction

In gratitude for God's guidance
through the Holy Spirit,
we will listen for direction
and seek to discern God's will.
We will give thanks each day
for the church on earth and the company of heaven,
for Holy Scripture and tradition.

Acknowledging that God's grace
is most often mediated through others
we will seek regular spiritual direction
from a person of holy wisdom.

When a suitable soul-friend is not available,
we will seek direction through good books,
family and friends, and our own prayer.

VI
Spiritual Reading

In response to God's call
to seek Him and grow in wisdom
we will attend to the Divine Word
spoken to us through scripture.
This will include study, but also taking to heart the Word
through meditating, praying and contemplating scripture.
Thus we come to know and love the person of Jesus Christ.
We will also seek insight by reading other writings
of spiritual significance.

VII
Eucharist

In thanksgiving
we will gather at Christ's table regularly,
receiving His Body and Blood
given to us for the life of the world.

The celebration of Eucharist
is central in the life of faith.

"The one who feeds on my flesh
and drinks my blood
remains in me, and I in him.
Just as the Father who has life sent me
and I have life because of the Father,
so the one who feeds on me
will have life because of me." *(Jn. 6:56-57)*

Green Bough Rule of Life

Christ offers himself to us in this sacrament
and we respond in obedience.
In receiving Christ
we become that which we receive,
the Body of Christ.
Taken, blessed, broken and distributed,
we are drawn into the mystery
of the paschal pattern of dying and rising.

In this sacrament
we anticipate the fullness of the kingdom
when all creation
will be gathered as one at Christ's table.
We will celebrate this hope each day
as we gather at table,
making each meal a remembrance of Christ's feast.

§

This rule is not meant to be a burden,
but is to enable us
to live the common life in Christ.
In our daily life in community
these disciplines must be lived.

It is here Christ calls us to be his body,
living in love, joy, peace,
patient endurance, kindness, generosity,
faith, gentleness and self-control.

A Particle of Light

It is here God gives us
our place among all the faithful.

"Therefore with angels and archangels,
and with all the company of heaven,
we laud and magnify thy glorious name,
evermore praising thee, and saying:

HOLY, HOLY, HOLY,
LORD GOD OF HOSTS:
HEAVEN AND EARTH
ARE FULL OF THY GLORY!
GLORY BE TO THEE,
O LORD MOST HIGH!
AMEN."

Green Bough Associates and Vowing Dates
(as of August 2018)

This story of Green Bough is laced with references,
named and unnamed, to our Associates.

Margaret Bullington (3/4/92)
Ralph Bailey (2/16/94)
Betty Voigt (6/20/94)
Martha Jane Petersen (2/5/95)
Elaine Eberhart (4/16/95)
Lisa W. Persons (4/7/96)
Alan Faulkner (5/26/96)
Ceci Duke (8/1/96)
Brian Wilcox (9/21/96)
Lucy Rose (2/2/97)
Ingrid Hauss (5/4/97)
Michael Hryniuk (5/4/97)
Lea Robinson (5/18/97)
Mary Ann Ramey (5/23/98)
Carla Roncoli (5/23/98)
Beth Knowlton (5/23/98)
Lynnsay Buehler (5/23/98)
Jimmy Asbell (9/8/98)
Ann Connor (5/25/99)
Beverly Elliott (9/11/99)
Betsy Caudill (1/16/00)
Stacey Simpson Duke (2/2/00)
Sophia Brothers Peterman (4/19/00)
Ginny Connelly (9/8/00)
Elizabeth Roles (1/15/01)
Barbara Luhn (9/8/01)
Gail Pitt (9/8/01)
Ellen Purdum (11/25/01)
Jill Oglesby Evans (1/1/02)
Barbara Dolan Meinert (5/31/02)

Linda Nelms (9/7/02)
Mary Alice Kemp (9/7/02)
Teresa Edwards (9/6/03)
Mimi Baird (10/24/03)
Chris Bean (2/14/04)
Joycelyn Trigg (3/27/04)
Hugh Grant (9/11/04)
Holly Shoaf-Okula (11/9/04)
Lesley Ann Drake (5/30/05)
Natallie Keiser (6/4/05)
Greg Loughlin (6/4/05)
Lalor Cadley (4/1/06)
Nan Ross (4/1/06)
June Kelly (5/17/06)
Becky Anne (9/7/07)
Maureen Casey (9/7/07)
Anne Sayre (1/1/08)
Kimberly Broerman (6/17/08)
Margaret Mathews (3/5/09)
Ingrid Hogan (5/31/09)
Sarah Carson (1/16/10)
Jo Marie Lyons (3/27/10)
Monirah Womack (9/24/11)
Susan Lupo (2/10/12)
Linda Bryant (8/24/12)
Vicki Tipps (10/16/12)
Barbara Pendergrast (12/12/12)
Wendy Farley (5/27/13)
Leslie Talbott (10/15/13)

Sally Nettles (6/6/14)
Beckie Bullard (6/15/14)
Holly Book (12/9/14)
Martha Wright (9/13/15)
Edith Woodling (2/25/16)
Tavye Morgan (4/5/16)
Ann Smith (5/31/16)
Kris Andersen (3/1/17)
Melanie Johnson (5/31/17)
Sharon Gregory (7/9/17)
JeffreAnn Sumrall (2/14/18)
Kay Hanson (5/21/18)
Ashley Hurst (7/9/18)
Kenneth Kelly (7/10/18)

Acknowledgements

I am deeply grateful for the exceptional people who guided, steadied and encouraged me through the writing of this memoir. Their generosity, beauty and *joie de vivre* made my heart sing as I wrote. I wish you could know each one of them.

I learned more about writing from my dear friend Louise Abbot than I could have learned in any college course. She generously shared the gifts of her gracious spirit and her writer's knowledge as she read my manuscript with love, understanding, and toughness. She put her arm around my shoulders and said with enthusiasm, "Yes, this is worth doing, and yes, you can do it." Along with her invaluable guidance, our frequent telephone visits were full of laughter, reflection, concern for our world and gratitude for our friendship. I hold her in my heart with love.

Dana Greene, lovely friend, somehow found time in the middle of her own busy writing schedule to read this manuscript. As a historian and biographer she made excellent suggestions for smoothing out some rough spots by ordering and clarifying names, dates and places. Our phone conversations and our notes also gave us good excuse for extra visiting and the joy of celebrating friendship.

My divinity school roommate Betty Hanigan deserves a gold medal for looking this over when it was still a pile of stories and memories stuffed in a manila folder. She had the grace to warn me that I should not try to tell *everything*. She has been a special friend and an uncanny guide for me ever since we first met at Duke in 1964.

June Kelly, sweet friend and Green Bough Associate, brought her exceptional skills as an English teacher to this project, polishing this work, curing it of punctuation ills, helping with chapter divisions and advising me on small adjustments that would make for a more graceful telling of this story. Her eagle eye and her great heart, along with her encouragement, all combined for wonderful help.

Thanks to Wendy Belkin, for the cover photograph of the night sky at Green Bough. Her videos can be found online. And my thanks to Margaret Mathews, exceptional watercolorist and chronicler of Green Bough scenes, for the watercolor of the Old House. Also, big thanks to Laura Nalesnik who turned these pages into a real book!

I give thanks for our family of Associates (whose names are listed earlier) who enlarge and enrich our lives; for Holly and Bob Book at Heartsong; for our Green Bough retreatants and for all who support us with love, prayer and gifts.

Several people have blessed me in special ways over the years: Michael Hryniuk, Ingrid Hauss, Jimmy and Vanda Asbell, Gail Pitt, Kim Boykin and Brian Mahan, Betsy Caudill, Joycelyn Trigg, Leslie Talbott, Sally Nettles, Martha Wright, Nancy Laurel Pettersen, Ted and Leslie Brelsford.

My love and deep gratitude to the following dear ones whose warmth and love have helped sustain me: Margaret and Elick Bullington, Lisa Persons, Lea Robinson, Lynnsay Buehler, Ann Connor, Elizabeth Roles, Barbara Luhn, Ellen Purdum, Jill Oglesby Evans, Barb Meinert, Lalor Cadley, Nan Ross, Kimberly Broerman, Barbara Pendergrast, Kenneth Kelly, Fran and John Shaw, Kay and Dave Hanson, Betty and Dave Voigt,

Rita Panciera, Rob Meeker, Curt Armstrong, Sandy Halperin, Dennis Berry and Virginia Merritt. And then there are those who have faithfully nipped at my heels, regularly holding me accountable, voicing concern for the project—"Are you writing?" "Write." "How's your writing going?" "Are you working on your memoir?" I name these holy hounds with gratitude: Brian Mahan, Cornelia Gamble, Linda Bryant, Vanessa Jackson, Vicki Tipps and Margaret Griffin. How I needed you all!

I am thankful for our Green Bough staff who care for houses and grounds. Kind, gifted Connie Weathersbee helps with all manner of things, including delicious, beautifully presented meals and expert upkeep of houses. Geneva Smith has been a loving presence here for many years, cleaning, doing laundry, helping in the kitchen, welcoming guests. The groundskeepers create an atmosphere of beauty for retreatants to enjoy. Steve Dixon, who helps in a variety of ways, has been with us longest, then Malcolm Wadley, chief mower, and Rob Cephas who helps part-time. J.T. Mincey helps with special building and repair projects. Matthew Thomas and Chris Milner are our newest helpers. These people are more than workers here, they are a part of the Green Bough family.

I am indebted to the Green Bough Board: Fran Shaw (one of the original members), Mary Alice Kemp, Rob Townes and newest member Beth Knowlton. I also remember here Joe Way who served on the Board until his death. They have taken seriously their oversight of this community—encouraging its growth, giving thoughtful guidance to its vision and keeping us all in their prayer.

I acknowledge with deep gratitude my beloved family—my parents, Martha and Woody, who gave me the best bringing-up imaginable; my brother Denny and sister-in-law Peggy who support me in countless ways; my stepmother Helen who encouraged me to write; Dennis, Brian and Karol, nephews and niece, of highest quality; and my great-nieces, Lainey, Evans and Etta whose faces have been before me as I have written down what I most want to 'tell the next generation'.

And what can I say about Steve Bullington and Oliver Ferrari? How I love these men! They are my 'dear'st of dear'sts'. I cannot even imagine what life would have been like without these two. Oliver, my Duke basketball buddy, who prays, loves the earth, makes me laugh, and whose many gifts I value highly, read this manuscript early and made helpful suggestions in sorting it out and shaving it down. He also put in many hours of tech support, never once making me feel like the computer dummy that I am—and he guided this project to fulfillment.

Steve, my treasured and trustworthy friend, my longstanding sidekick and bulgy bear (ask if you want to know more), my comrade for the journey, my soulmate, has signed off on the history and memories in this account. His daily presence, prayer, music, liturgical gifts, tireless work and unwavering love have borne me up through the years at Green Bough. These two men are like fire-tried gold. They can be turned to in need. Our life together as a community of prayer has made us intimate companions. To them, all my thanks!

And you, dear reader (I've been waiting for a place to use those words), you who have this memoir in hand, may you find here a word intended just for you. Your reading engages us in conversation, which I pray will spill over into the lives of others. "You are the light of the world!"

Notes

Prologue

1. Gabriel Marcel, *Philosophy of Existentialism*, (Copyright 1956, CitadelPress re-issue edition, 2002), 95.
2. Matthew 5:14, 16 (NRSV).

Chapter 1

1. Psalm 139:13-16a (NRSV).
2. Genesis 1:1, 3-4, 31.
3. Isaiah 46:3 (NRSV).
4. Psalm 130:1 (NRSV).

Chapter 2

1. Isaiah 43:1 (NRSV).
2. John Wesley, Sermon 39, "Catholic Spirit."
3. John 20:1 (NRSV).
4. Christopher Fry, *A Sleep of Prisoners*, (New York, Oxford University Press, 1954), 49.

Chapter 3

1. D. H. Lawrence, "Song of a Man Who Has Come Through", *Selected Poems*, (Viking Press, 1959), 74.

Chapter 4

1. Genesis 30:1.

Chapter 5

1. Psalm 110:3 (The Grail Psalms).

Chapter 8

1. Psalm 16:6.
2. St. Teresa of Avila, prayer written in her Breviary.
3. Johannes B. Metz, *Poverty of Spirit,* (Paulist Press), 74.
4. John 1:5 (NRSV).
5. Luke 1:78-79 (New American Bible).
6. Malachi 3:2-3.
7. Genesis 45.

Chapter 10

1. Isaiah 62:4 (NRSV).
2. John LaFarge, *The Manner is Ordinary*, (Doubleday & Company, 1957), 108.

Chapter 11

1. Steve Bullington, *Green Bough Newsletter*, 1988.
2. Psalm 131:1-2, (New American Bible).
3. Song of Solomon 2:4 (NRSV).
4. Luke 10:38-42.
5. John 21:11-18.
6. Psalm 63:7.
7. Oliver Ferrari, *Green Bough Newsletter*, 2017.
8. Psalm 24:1.

Chapter 12

1. Pierre Teilhard de Chardin, *The Divine Milieu*, (Harper & Rowe, New York, 1960), 107.
2. Mark 4:31 (NRSV).
3. Proverbs 29:18 (King James Version).
4. Psalm 57:7-8 (The Grail Psalms).
5. Exodus 13:19 (NRSV).
6. Martin Buber, *Daniel: Dialogues on Realization*, (Holt, Rinehart and Winston, 1964), 95.

Chapter 13

1. See Ephesians 2.
2. Luke 2:29-30 (New American Bible).

Chapter 14

1. *Raissa's Journal*, presented by Jacques Maritain, (Magi Books, Inc., Albany, New York), 151-155.
2. Leviticus 23:10.
3. Robert Ellsberg, *All Saints: Daily Reflections on Saints, Prophets, and Witnesses for our Time*, (The Crossroad Publishing Company, New York 1997), 433.
4. Luke 1:35 (NRSV).
5. Matthew 18:20 (NRSV).
6. Joyce Rupp, *Dear Heart, Come Home*, (The Crossroad Publishing Company, New York, 1996), 99.
7. Jeremiah 17:7-8 (NRSV).

Chapter 15

1. John Wesley's Covenant Service, "An Order of Worship for Such As Would Enter into or Renew Their Covenant with God," *The Book of Worship for Church and Home,* The United Methodist Church, (The United Methodist Publishing House, Nashville, Tennessee, 1964), 387.
2. See Hebrews 4:12-13.
3. Psalm 121:8 (New American Bible).
4. Romans 11:33 (NRSV).
5. Henri J.M. Nouwen, *Clowning in Rome: Reflections on Solitude, Celibacy, Prayer, and Contemplation,* (Image Books, 1979), 88.

Chapter 16

1. II Timothy 1:12.

Postlude

1. Psalm 110:3 (The Grail Psalms).
2. Psalm 84:6 (NRSV).
3. Psalm 34:8 (NRSV).
4. Psalm 122:8-9.

Made in the USA
Columbia, SC
26 January 2023